TALES, TRIVIA AND RAMBLING ROUTES FOR HIKERS

WALK

WALK

An Hachette UK Company
www.hachette.co.uk

Summersdale Publishers Ltd
Part of Octopus Publishing Group Limited
Carmelite House
50 Victoria Embankment
LONDON
EC4Y 0DZ
UK

www.summersdale.com

Printed and bound in Poland

ISBN: 978-1-78685-259-5

Substantial discounts on bulk quantities of Summersdale books are available to corporations, professional associations and other organisations. For details contact general enquiries: telephone: +44 (0) 1243 756902 or email: enquiries@summersdale.com.

TALES, TRIVIA AND RAMBLING ROUTES FOR HIKERS

WALK

DAVID BATHURST

summersdale

CONTENTS

INTRODUCTION

'Walking is the best possible exercise.
Habituate yourself to walk very far.'

Thomas Jefferson

Putting one foot in front of the other is one of the most natural of human activities. Most of us will, in the course of a day, do all sorts of walking – walking downstairs to breakfast in the morning, walking to the car, the bus stop or the railway station, walking to work or class, walking between offices and lecture theatres, popping down to the pub or the corner shop, taking your dog out – purposeful, yes, but borne of necessity.

This book is about walking, not for necessity, but for pleasure, enjoyment, satisfaction and happiness – a celebration of walking not because you're constrained to do it by the daily round but because you actually want to do it. We hope that this book will help you to appreciate walking for what it is – an infinitely rewarding pastime that will provide you with interest and enjoyment throughout your life.

In these pages you'll learn about:

- The benefits to you, and others, of walking (Chapter 1)
- The history of walking for leisure (Chapter 2)
- Getting started – basic and easy walking (Chapter 3)
- How to get serious as a walker – wilder walking (Chapter 4)
- The challenges of long-distance walking (Chapter 5)
- Some remarkable and courageous – and very speedy – walkers (Chapter 6)

So read on – but don't expect to finish the book. For hopefully within a few pages you'll have tightened your laces and be off down the road towards the nearest public footpath...

1 | WHY WALK?

'Walk and be happy, walk and be healthy.'

Charles Dickens

'The gym experience is not for everyone. Salvation comes in the form of a good old-fashioned walk.'

Clare Balding

Walking is often called the perfect exercise. It's remarkable that something so simple can be so restorative, therapeutic and utterly rewarding in so many ways. In this section we look at why walking for enjoyment is great.

Walking is good for your health: the Ancient Greek physician Hippocrates described walking as 'man's best medicine'. In our day there's a wealth of scientific evidence to show that regular walking helps to reduce the risk of many diseases and symptoms of ill health...

- Stress
- High blood pressure
- Raised levels of cholesterol
- Heart disease
- Strokes
- Some forms of cancer
- Type 2 diabetes*

... and enhances:
- Mood
- Self-esteem

*Research by George Washington University suggests that a 15-minute walk after meals could help reduce the risk of developing Type 2 diabetes.

Here are some reported benefits from people who've come to enjoy walking through the Walking for Health walking schemes, of which there are currently over 400:

- Feeling happy and energised

- Having more stamina

- Living longer, feeling fitter, enjoying life

- Keeping fit and independent in retirement

- Being able to enjoy life to the full

- Having a good, healthy heart, normal blood pressure and good circulation

Experts from Saarland University in Germany reported to the European Society of Cardiology Congress in 2015 that just 25 minutes of walking a day can add up to seven years to your life.

Did you know that studies on the brains of older people have shown that keeping physically active can improve cognitive function, memory, attention and processing speed, and reduce the risk of cognitive decline and dementia?

A new concept, 'Walks on Prescription', has recently been established, which sees doctors refer patients for walking programmes over a period of several weeks. With less than half of Americans getting their recommended amount of daily exercise, the concept of 'walking prescriptions' is gaining wider adoption at medical practices around the US as a viable alternative to traditional medicines.

The UK government, in recommending we all do at least 30 minutes of physical activity five times a week, suggests brisk walking as one form of activity. Studies show that people who choose to walk at least part of the way to work are more productive, happier and take less time off sick.

Did you know that walking is a great calorie burner?
A 42-minute walk can walk off a pint of lager/ale.
A 56-minute walk can walk off a hot dog with white roll.
But it takes 2 hours 9 minutes to walk off a steak pie.
And almost 6 hours to walk off the 1,758 calories in a Dairy Milk Easter egg!

WALKING ENHANCES CREATIVITY

Walking has been described as an all-round lift for the mind, body and soul, its regular rhythm helping creativity to blossom in the mind. Charles Dickens, the prolific nineteenth-century author, was a really keen walker and recorded in his diaries how he would go on 20-mile (32-km) walks to conceive the plots of his novels. Louisa May Alcott was out walking when the idea for *Little Women*, one of the best-loved children's novels of all time, came to her, and she remembers that she could hardly wait to get home and start work on it. It was walking in the Malvern Hills in Worcestershire that inspired the great British composer Edward Elgar to write some of his most famous works, and those same hills gave similar inspiration to the novelist J. R. R. Tolkien and the poets William Langland and W. H. Auden. Charlotte Brontë clearly knew the value of a good walk; the first ten words of her novel *Jane Eyre*, one of the greatest novels of all time, express the eponymous heroine's regret that 'There was no possibility of taking a walk that day.' In the modern age, walking helps you escape the computer screen and gives you space to think through new projects.

WALKING ENHANCES YOUR SOCIAL LIFE

The author Mark Twain wrote that 'the true charm of pedestrianism does not lie in the walking, or in the scenery, but in the talking.' Many people, among them BBC sports presenter Clare Balding, enjoy walking as a social activity. The popularity of walkers' clubs, which will be explored in greater detail later in this book, shows that there is something special and fulfilling in sharing a walking experience with someone else and making new friends as a result of a common interest in walking.

WALKING CAN HELP OTHERS

Charity walking has increased massively in popularity in recent years. Many people, wanting to raise money for a worthy cause, have opted for sponsored walks, asking family and friends to pledge a certain sum for every mile walked or on successful completion. There's no reason why you can't organise your own. Some charities now organise specific events, bringing together large numbers of people to take on a walking challenge and asking the entrants to seek sponsorship. The British Heart Foundation in the UK, for example, organised a London to Oxford trek in May 2017 consisting of a non-stop walk of 100 km. The British Heart Foundation are also organising a number of charity walking treks overseas in 2018, including the Great Wall Of China, Machu Picchu in Peru, the Himalayas and an Icelandic Lava Trek.

Other recent charity challenges with an individual twist include:

A cockney-themed London marathon walk ('ball of chalk') in September 2017 including lessons in cockney rhyming slang – 'You can expect tired pins and plates of meat!'

Just Walk event at Goodwood in West Sussex in May 2017 involving raising money for a range of charities and the choice of walking between 10 km (6.25 miles) and a massive 60 km (37.5 miles) in one day.

Macmillan Mighty Hike – one-day hiking marathons in aid of Macmillan Cancer Care, in locations including Loch Lomond and the Lake District during the summer of 2017.

Many of the 'ultimate' walks, described later in this book, have been undertaken in order to raise money for charity. For instance, John Merrill's walk round the entire coastline of Great Britain, accomplished in 1978, raised more than £40,000 for the Royal Commonwealth Society for the Blind.

Did you know that in April 1988 the English Test cricketer Ian Botham re-enacted the exploits of Hannibal and walked 500 miles (800 km) from Perpignan to Turin across the Alps with a troop of elephants, all in aid of leukaemia research?

WALKING IS EDUCATIONAL

Even a short walk can give you a valuable history or geography lesson or tell you about the wildlife and plant life in the locality. Walking gives you the time to take things in and enjoy them, unlike a journey by car, bus or train, or even bicycle, where the scenery can whizz past without your appreciating any of it. Despite modern building and road development, which have lost us so many acres of precious countryside and historic landmarks, just walking a mile from your doorstep, whether in an urban or rural environment, will almost certainly put you in touch with the past, some interesting or picturesque geographical phenomenon, or an area of grassland or woodland which supports a variety of plants, insects or even animals. We may even find sources of food such as edible fungi, flora and seaweed, not to mention the ever-popular blackberry (going out blackberry picking is a great reason for walking in August and September!). We are blessed in Great Britain with a massive number of historic churches; it's likely that there will be one such church just a short walk from you, and whatever your religious inclination, entering and exploring the church will kindle your spirit and provide you with a fascinating insight into community life, past and present.

Even just looking around you as you walk can be an education in itself. Although our unpredictable British weather can be a nuisance, it provides an endless variety of cloudscapes. The wonderful book by Gavin Pretor-Pinney, *The Cloudspotter's Guide*, is great for explaining the difference between the rippling mackerel cirrocumulus skies and the nimbostratus, promising rain. You can become a weather forecaster just by walking! Pretor-Pinney has also written, more recently, *The Wave-Watcher's Companion* for those wanting to learn more from a seaside stroll. A more general guide to the often unnoticed phenomena around us is Tristan Gooley's *The Walker's Guide to Outdoor Clues and Signs*. You may become so engrossed by what you see that you never venture more than a few hundred yards from your front door!

On the other hand, having tasted the educational value of a short walk from your doorstep, you may want to spread your wings and go further afield, perhaps travelling by car, bus or train to savour the historic, architectural, geographical or wildlife highlights of other areas, or joining an organised city or wildlife walk.

WALKING IS AN ADVENTURE

There's something romantic and intimate about travelling on foot. In no other means of transport are you closer to what's actually going on around you. What's more, you're not dependent on a vehicle – you are entirely dependent on yourself and your ability to propel yourself.

Did you know that in 2010, Ed Stafford became the first man to walk the entire length of the Amazon; his two-and-a-half-year journey saw him confronting alligators, jaguars, pit vipers and machete-wielding tribesmen. A British Army officer, Levison Wood, undertook the first ever expedition to walk the entire length of the River Nile in Africa, over nine months in 2013/14. He followed that up in 2015 by walking the whole length of the Himalayas. He has gone on to walk the entire length of Central America from Mexico to Colombia, a total of 1,800 miles (2,880 km), which was made into a 2017 Channel 4 series *Walking the Americas.* He then walked and hitch-hiked the 2,600 miles (4,160 km) from Russia to Iran, also televised by Channel 4 in 2017.

Many famous figures, who have distinguished themselves principally in other fields, have embarked on walking adventures during their lives.

LAURIE LEE

Laurie Lee was born in 1914 and died in 1997. Setting out in 1934 from his Cotswold home, Lee walked first to London then sailed to Spain, walking across that country from north to south and scraping a living by playing his violin outside street cafes. His adventure is recounted in his 1969 book *As I Walked Out One Midsummer Morning*.

Having completed his walk through Spain, he volunteered in the Spanish Civil War but his service was cut short by epilepsy and he returned to England. Lee became a journalist and scriptwriter, and during World War Two he made documentary films and became publications editor for the Ministry of Information. It was in 1959 that he published the work for which he became most famous, *Cider With Rosie*, about his childhood in Slad, Gloucestershire, where he returned in later life. It took him two years and three drafts to complete the memoir.

'I was tasting the extravagant quality of being free.'

Laurie Lee, *As I Walked Out One Midsummer Morning*

*'I followed this straight southern track for several days...
There was really no hurry. I was going nowhere.'*

Laurie Lee, *As I Walked Out One Midsummer Morning*

ERIC NEWBY

Eric Newby was born in 1919 and died in 2006. His taste for adventure was demonstrated when he was just 19 by a sea voyage from Australia to Europe via Cape Horn. He was awarded the Military Cross for his part in the Allied raid on Sicily in August 1942. His book, *A Short Walk in the Hindu Kush*, was the written account of his adventure in the Nuristan mountains of Afghanistan, and was described by the American novelist Rick Skwiot as being told with 'understatement, self-effacement, savage wit, honed irony and unrelenting honesty'. In 1963 he was made travel editor for the *Observer* newspaper and was subsequently given a Lifetime Achievement Award of the British Guild of Travel Writers.

PATRICK LEIGH FERMOR

Patrick Leigh Fermor was born in 1915 and died in 2011. He was just 18 when he decided to walk across Europe from Hook of Holland to Constantinople, arriving at his destination two years later. He took with him little more than a few clothes, letters of introduction, and some books of poetry. He slept in barns and shepherds' huts but was also invited into many country houses owned by the aristocracy. His adventures are recounted in *A Time of Gifts* and *Between the Woods and the Water*. Fermor then spent some years travelling about the more remote parts of Greece on foot and by mule. During World War Two he belonged to the Special Operations Executive, playing a prominent part in the Cretan Resistance. He was described by a BBC journalist as a 'cross between Indiana Jones, James Bond and Graham Greene.' He was knighted in 2004, having previously received the DSO and OBE.

WALKING GIVES YOU ACCESS ALL AREAS

Not quite all, but moving in that direction. Later in the book we'll look at the so-called 'right to roam' – to walk in the UK countryside wherever you wish, subject to certain obvious restrictions, e.g. national security – which is already available in Scotland and which also applies to many areas of England and Wales. Different countries have different laws in relation to access to the countryside – check what rights you have before you travel. But even where the right to roam is restricted, walkers can reach parts of the countryside that are quite inaccessible to motorists or even cyclists or horse-riders.

---

*'I am monarch of all I survey; my right
there is none to dispute.'*

William Cowper

---

*Writer and experienced walker H. D. Westacott said
that while by the roadside there was always the smell of
petrol fumes, 'two hundred yards away over the stile it is
possible to smell the wild fragrance of the countryside.'*

(*The Walker's Handbook, 1978 edition*)

It's true that many roads, even major roads, can take the motor traveller through magnificent scenery, but by their very nature they cannot provide a pollution-free countryside experience. And while many footpaths can be and are used by cyclists, a very great number of them are for walkers only – where walkers alone can savour a remoteness and peace, uncluttered by reminders of the modern, ephemeral and temporal world. Moreover, through punishing terrain the cyclist will always be mindful of the potential damage to his or her machine and the possibility of mechanical breakdown. A walker has none of these concerns and can enjoy a variety of scenic experiences that is unparalleled by any other form of transport. Arguably the best is a hilltop. There is something particularly special about walking to a summit and gazing down on the landscape below, which may be rural, a seemingly endless patchwork of fields, dotted with villages and farmsteads, or may provide a bird's-eye view of one of our great cities. The good news is that you don't need to have the mountaineering skills of Sir Edmund Hillary and you don't require ice axes or crampons to appreciate the beauty of the British landscape.

SIX EXPERIENCES FOR WALKERS ONLY!

- A ridgetop march in a Cumbrian mountain range

- Climbing to the highest point in England (Scafell Pike, Cumbria)

- A coastal walk over the cliffs of Cornwall

- A beachcombing walk

- Bog-trotting across Dartmoor

- A woodland walk on Exmoor

Each one brings its own atmosphere, surroundings, colours, aromas, and joys – just for the walker.

*'The whole object of travel is not to set foot on foreign land –
it is at last to set foot on one's own country as a foreign land.'*

G. K. Chesterton

WALKING IS FULFILLING

Later in this book you will read of some walkers who have achieved great things, from walking the coastline of Great Britain to walking right round the world. Their motives will have varied, but they did it, at least in part, because they wanted to tell themselves they could. In the same way, whether you walk for others or for yourself, you can learn much about yourself, your inner strength, your self-discipline and resolve, through walking, whether because of the nature of terrain, the distance you're covering or in conquering any physical or psychological fears you may have.

Alfred Wainwright, whom we'll meet again later in this book, wrote of conquering the Pennine Way, one of the biggest walking challenges in Britain:

*'You do it because you count it a personal
achievement. Which it is, precisely.'*

Alfred Wainwright, *Pennine Way Companion*

If you think 'just walking' is unproductive or unable to stir the soul, you could always be doing something else at the same time. Here are just a few wacky walking records set recently...

- Doug McManaman walked 3,050 yds (2,790 m) while balancing an egg on the back of his hand in Cumberland County, Nova Scotia, Canada on 9 June 2014.

- A total of 448 people participated in a photography walk, the largest of its kind on record, in Chandigarh in India on 26 September 2015.

- 'Cooljuggler' walked over five people while juggling five lit firetorches in Long Beach, California, USA, on 13 February 2016 (don't try this at home!).

- Satpal Kuntal walked on his hands for 2 minutes, 49.34 seconds at Ahmednagar, Maharashtra, India on 27 March 2016.

- Michael McCastle walked 22 miles (35 km) in 24 hours while pulling a 2.2-ton Ford truck in Death Valley, California, USA on 23 May 2016.

- Pavol Durdik threw and caught an apple 286 times while walking forward in an apple orchard in Puchov, Slovakia on 15 October 2016.

- Mike Hout walked backwards for 60 yds (55 m) while juggling three bowling balls in Miamisburg, Ohio, USA on 2 December 2016.

AND THE GREAT NEWS IS, WALKING NEEDN'T COST ANYTHING

In difficult economic times, walking is particularly brilliant because it is free. If you're starting your walk from home, the only financial outlay required for the walking itself is a weatherproof coat and some comfortable shoes – but you may have those already. It is true that if you go on a guided walk there may be a fee to pay or the expectation of a gratuity to your leader at the end, but if you go walking independently, whether on our own, or with companions, it will cost you nothing. Unlike many outdoor activities, you need no special training or tuition (although later in the book we'll look at what you *will* need in order to develop as a walker). You can start now! You do not need the fitness and stamina levels required for running or other energetic sports such as football or tennis. You can continue to enjoy it at any age. Once you start walking, it is only tiredness in your legs or feet that will compel you to stop. The body has a remarkable ability to keep going and support you no matter how far you choose to walk.

Now let's see how it all started…

2 | WALKING FOR ENJOYMENT

'Away we went in jubilant mood, determined to carry out the assault on Kinder Scout.'

Benny Rothman's memories of the Kinder Trespass as quoted in Sinclair McKay's book *Ramble On*

It may seem incongruous that in an age obsessed by technology and other sophisticated forms of entertainment, the simple pastime of walking is so popular. And even more incongruously, perhaps, it is only in the comparatively recent past that walking for pleasure has become the boom industry that it undoubtedly now is.

Did you know that a survey conducted by the UK walkers' organisation the Ramblers in 2010 revealed that 9.1 million adults in England, or 22 per cent of the population, walk recreationally for at least every 30 minutes every month, and around 63 per cent of adults walk recreationally at least once a year. Also in 2010 it was found that the number of Americans who took a walk for pleasure at least once a week had risen by six per cent in five years to 62 per cent.

WALKING BECOMES FUN

Paths have been with us since prehistoric times, but not for leisure reasons. They were established for trading purposes and linked centres where essentials of prehistoric life were to be found. A classic example of a prehistoric trading route is the Great Ridgeway, which linked Lyme Regis in Dorset with Hunstanton in Norfolk, the route serving as a drove road, a trading route, and a convenient track for invaders. Though some routes, previously trading routes, were used by pilgrims, e.g. between Winchester and Canterbury, these paths were never intended, or used, for enjoyment. During the Middle Ages paths became used as a means of getting about the countryside by the shortest route. Although people might enjoy a stroll around a park or garden for leisure, or 'take the air' for health reasons, as recently as the eighteenth century rambling for pleasure was virtually unheard of in Britain. In 1782 a German pastor, Carl Moritz, commented that the pedestrian in Britain seems to be: 'considered as a sort of wild man or an out-of-the-way being who is stared at, pitied, suspected and shunned by everybody who meets him'.

It was only towards the end of the eighteenth and into the nineteenth century that paths began to be used for recreational purposes, a welcome relief from polluted environments and the strains of daily life brought about by the Industrial Revolution. The novels of Thomas Hardy and Jane Austen have many references to recreational walks on public paths. The poet William Wordsworth and his contemporary, Samuel Taylor Coleridge, were both keen walkers; the essayist William Hazlitt walked with Coleridge and although he claimed he couldn't see the virtue of walking and talking at the same time he wrote: 'Give me the blue sky over my head, and the green turf beneath my feet, a winding road before me, and three hours' march to dinner... '

A VERY SHORT HISTORY OF WALKING FOR FUN IN THE NINETEENTH CENTURY

1810   publication of Wordsworth's *Guide To The Lakes*, springing from his love of walking in the Lake District

1820s   establishment of first ramblers' clubs in Britain

1833   formation of Select Committee on Public Walks

1854   publication of Hugh MacDonald's *Rambles Round Glasgow*

1884   Scotsman James Bryce tries (unsuccessfully) to make an Access to Mountains Bill become law

1892   formation of West of Scotland Ramblers' Alliance, Britain's first rambling federation

Did you know that it's estimated that Wordsworth had walked some 180,000 miles (288,000 km) by the age of 65?

Did you know that the first walk from Land's End to John o'Groats was undertaken in September 1871 by Robert and John Naylor, wealthy brothers from Cheshire. They were inspired to do the end-to-end walk by reading literature about walks to Land's End from London and to John o'Groats from London. It took them eight days just to get to the start, as they began by sailing to the Shetlands, sailing from there to Thurso and walking from Thurso to the start. They said they did this to avoid repeating anything! Displaying very impressive levels of fitness, they averaged 25 miles (40 km) a day and their complete end-to-end walk was 1,372 miles (2,195 km) in length. They never walked on Sundays. It took them nine weeks to complete the journey.

During the nineteenth century, rambling clubs continued to be established in northern England and the popularity of rambling was still growing in the early years of the twentieth century. During the inter-war years, thousands of unemployed people left the industrial cities of the north every weekend, walking the hills of Derbyshire, Northumberland and Yorkshire. By the early 1930s, a number of walkers' federations had been formed and in 1931 six regional federations representing walkers from across Britain created the National Council of

Ramblers' Federations. The walking movement was gaining momentum!

But – and it was a big but – the interests of walkers were still in fierce competition with private landowners closing off their land and refusing public access to it. The huge network of signed and mapped footpaths and bridleways we enjoy today simply didn't exist. Walkers at that time wanted more – much more – access. Landowners dug in their heels.

The battle lines were drawn...

THE KINDER TRESPASS

One of the most popular areas for recreational walking at this time was the Peak District in Derbyshire. From the late 1890s climbers were turning their attention to the gritstone edges of the northern part of the Peak District, the so-called Dark Peak area, with bog-trotting – the traversing of tough sections of moorland – proving increasingly popular. By the 1930s some weekends saw as many as 10,000 walkers in the area. However, walkers found themselves frustrated at the lack of access to large parts of the moor. On 24 April 1932 around 500 walkers decided to make a stand against this. They assembled at the small town of Hayfield, a gateway to the Dark Peak, and set off into prohibited territory in peaceful protest. A group of gamekeepers met them, fighting broke out, the police intervened and as a result, a number were prosecuted and five spent time in prison. But their efforts were not in vain. The protestors excited massive support and sympathy from those who wanted greater access to our wonderful countryside.

THE RAMBLERS

It was less than three years after the Kinder Trespass that the Ramblers' Association (later the Ramblers) was founded to represent the interests of recreational walkers at national level.

THINGS YOU MAY NOT KNOW ABOUT THE RAMBLERS

- The association was officially created on 1 January 1935.

- By 1936 it had 1,200 members; in 2017 it had 123,000 members.

- Throughout its existence the Ramblers' Association (the Ramblers) has campaigned for increased access to the countryside.

- It was instrumental in the establishment of National Parks and National Trails.

- Every year, its volunteers lead in the region of 30,000 group walks, attracting over half a million ramblers.

- In 2017, its president was the broadcaster Stuart Maconie; previously it was well-known TV presenter Julia Bradbury.

- The Ramblers have campaigned robustly to secure public access to the coast in Wales and England, and in May 2012 achieved a notable victory with the opening of the complete Wales Coast Path.

- In recent years they have been campaigning for the preservation and safeguarding of the National Trails, the official long-distance footpaths, in Britain.

- The Ramblers secured £5 million of government funding for the purpose of creating a path round the whole coastline of England; it is hoped that the complete path will open as a National Trail in 2020.

- In 2007, they launched a Get Walking, Keep Walking project in England aimed at helping inactive people in the inner cities to walk independently through a 12-week walking programme. This project received a lottery grant and is estimated to have helped over 100,000 people.

- The Ramblers' aims are to promote walking, safeguard paths, increase access for walkers, protect the countryside and educate the public.

During World War Two, a blueprint for National Parks and greater access to the countryside was laid down and these objectives were realised by the most important piece of legislation for recreational walkers ever enacted: The National Parks and Access to Countryside Act 1949.

This Act proposed:

- Setting up of a National Parks Commission

- A framework for defining rights of way

- Access agreements with landowners to give free access to open country

- The establishment of long-distance footpaths

NATIONAL PARKS

The concept of National Parks sounds modern but the first National Park in the world, Yellowstone in the USA, was established in 1872. It was 'dedicated and set apart as a public park or pleasuring ground for the benefit and enjoyment of the people.' Years before that, William Wordsworth had a similar vision for his beloved Lake District. Numerous bills were laid before British parliament during the early part of the twentieth century to improve public access to areas of outstanding beauty, but none were successful. It was only during World War Two that an architect, John Dower, was commissioned to write a report with a view to the establishment of National Parks, which in 1942 were stated to be long overdue. John Dower defined a National Park in this way:

> *'An extensive area of beautiful and relatively
> wild country in which...*
> *The characteristic landscape beauty is strictly preserved*
> *Access and facilities for public open-air enjoyment [are]
> amply provided*
> *Wildlife and places of architectural and historic interest [are]
> suitably protected*
> *Established farming use is effectively maintained.'*

John Dower

The 1949 Act provided a legislative framework for establishing the National Parks. Twelve areas in the United Kingdom were proposed for National Park status and all subsequently achieved it, ten of them during the 1950s. The ownership of the land didn't change: for each an executive committee was appointed, responsible for regulating development within the National Park and providing amenities for visitors.

National Parks have proved one of the great success stories in the history of walking for pleasure. Assisted by tight controls on development, preserving rights of access, protection of wildlife and habitats, and characterised by immense beauty and the individual character of each one, the concept of the National Park is still thriving today. They provide some of the best opportunities for challenging and rewarding walking in Great Britain. We'll look at them, and also National Parks around the world, in greater detail later in this book.

ACCESS TO THE COUNTRYSIDE

The 1949 Act laid upon local authorities a statutory duty to compile and publish Definitive Maps showing all public paths on a scale not less than 1:25,000 (the scale of the Ordnance Survey Explorer Maps). Where there was a dispute as to whether a path was a public right of way or not, the first resort was negotiation and, if that failed to resolve the issue, there would be a public inquiry and a final decision would be taken by the Minister of Town and Country Planning. The importance of the Definitive Map was huge, because it conclusively proved that something shown as a right of way was a right of way – even if it was included by mistake! – and legislation ensured that the local authority had the duty to keep it open, only diverting or extinguishing it by due legal process, and landowners had to ensure that its course remained (and remains) unobstructed.

The law also allows for new paths to be created, but the authorities responsible for authorising such a path must bear in mind the effect on the rights of those interested in the land. The number of creation orders is small. There are also so-called permissive paths which aren't public footpaths as such but where the landowner allows the public to use a path subject to his right to impose limitations and withdraw permission in certain circumstances.

Did you know that there are about 100,000 miles (160,000 km) of public paths in England and Wales?

Although this all sounds good news to walkers, the Ramblers wanted more – the so-called right to roam in England and Wales.

THE RIGHT TO ROAM

This was the right to unhindered access to open country – although not, obviously, private property or cultivated land. Despite the proposal in the 1949 Act of arrangements for 'free access', ramblers had to wait until the Countryside and Rights of Way Act 2000 (known as CROW) for the implementation of rights to roam in open country in England and Wales. Not that this Act provided unlimited rights: rights were implemented region by region and not all uncultivated land was covered by the legislation.

RIGHT TO ROAM Q & A 1

Q What might be considered open/uncultivated country?
A Moorland
   Mountains
   Heathland
   Downland
   Woodland
   The coast

In Scotland this right was already available. So if, for instance, before the year 2000 you wanted to walk the coastline of Great

Britain, you'd be able to walk as near as you liked to the shoreline in Scotland, but you'd be forced to use the nearest right of way to the coast in England and Wales. This meant you'd often have to stay some way back from the shoreline. Although the 'right to roam' was available in Scotland even before 2000, it was given statutory recognition by the Land Reform (Scotland) Act 2003, confirming unhindered access to open country in Scotland. If you look at a large-scale Ordnance Survey map of any part of Scotland you'll see that there are no footpaths marked on it. This is because in Scotland everyone has access rights in law over land, providing the rights are exercised responsibly in accordance with the Scottish Outdoor Access Code.

RIGHT TO ROAM Q & A 2

Q So how do you know where you can roam in England and Wales?

A As each particular piece of open country acquired the right to roam provision it was designated as 'access land' and shown as such on the larger-scale Ordnance Survey maps. The newer Explorer maps show where access land can be found, using a distinctive brown-shaded boundary. Woodlands are marked with either a pale green for access land or a darker shade of green for areas not designated as access land.

The significance of access land is huge. It means that while you're in the access land, you're not restricted to public footpaths. You can walk anywhere, as in Scotland!

Of course, the right to roam is subject to obvious restrictions such as non-interference with important countryside activity (such as farming), not endangering the life of the countryside, and following the Countryside Code, which is set out in Chapter 3.

LONG-DISTANCE PATHS

The vision of the 1949 Act for long-distance footpaths became a reality. The first to open was the Pennine Way in 1965. The Pennine Way was the brainchild of Tom Stephenson, sometime secretary of the Ramblers Association, who, by what John Hillaby described as 'dogged bargaining, barter and compromise', negotiated with landowners to create a continuous right of way across the Pennines – the southern end of which crossed the very land into which the Kinder Trespassers had dared to enter back in 1932. A number of other officially-designated long-distance routes now exist in Great Britain, together with a vast number of 'named' long-distance paths. For more information on long-distance walking routes, see Chapter 5.

Nowadays walking for pleasure is thriving. Just a glance at the internet will show you how many walkers' clubs there are; most towns now boast at least one shop specialising in the sale of outdoor goods for walkers; there are several magazines devoted to walking for pleasure; Julia Bradbury's UK television series and books, including *Unforgettable Walks* and her books of

Railway Walks and *Wainwright Walks*, have enjoyed and continue to enjoy huge popularity; new technology, with digital walking guides and apps, has enabled described walks of all levels of length and difficulty to become available at the touch of a button; and social media allows experiences, including photos, of great walks to be shared and discussed on Facebook and Instagram and other platforms.

Walking has never been more popular and never been easier to take up seriously.

So now it's your turn...

3 | GETTING STARTED – EASY WALKING FOR PLEASURE

'Travelling on foot can be meditative,
fostering a slow frame of mind.'

Carl Honoré, *In Praise of Slow*

Walking for pleasure isn't like learning a musical instrument or a sport. It is literally possible to start by putting down this book (or whatever else you happen to be doing) and setting off. It really is that easy.

That said, if you're to enjoy walking, it's important that you aren't put off by things going wrong during your first few walks for pleasure, whether they're a retirement hobby or a post-Sunday-lunch stroll.

WALKERS' WOES

- ◆ You get lost
- ◆ You get wet or muddy
- ◆ You get too hot or too cold
- ◆ You get thirsty or hungry
- ◆ You wear yourself out
- ◆ You get sore feet or blisters

You can avoid all these common afflictions if you plan a little and think a little – and indeed all of the avoidance techniques set out below hold good for all your walking for pleasure in future.

BE PREPARED...

Avoid getting lost – by basing your initial walks from your home, where you'll be familiar with the local area, and sticking to the roads, paths and tracks you know. There'll be plenty of time to be more adventurous once you've got more experienced. Using familiar walkways obviates the need to read a map and avoids any risk of trespass. You'll appreciate the surroundings more as well. If you live or are staying in a seaside town, you'll be hugely blessed, as you can follow the promenade or the beach (being careful to watch the tide!); again, good, easy walking that poses no navigational difficulty, and with the bonus of sea views and good sea air. Similarly, there may be areas of woodland in your area with well-marked and firm forest trails. If you're able to read a map there's no reason why you can't be more adventurous, but early on it's better to stick with what you know, and as your map-reading skills improve (see Chapter 4) you can become a little bolder!

Another way to avoid getting lost is to go out with companions who know the way, or on a guided walk. To find out what guided walks are on offer in your locality, just check with your nearest tourist information office. Walking organisations as a means of getting into more ambitious walking are discussed at the end of the chapter.

Avoid getting wet – by making sure you go walking when it's dry and forecast to stay that way for however long you're out. While long-range forecasting is notoriously inaccurate (never believe the sensationalist press headlines prophesying the 'hottest summer on record on the way/coldest winter on record on the way'), short-range forecasts are generally very reliable and experience indicates that it's very rare indeed for it to rain following a forecast of dry weather. Walking in the rain can be fun, but getting wet through is no fun at all. Of course, if you're going out on a longer, 'serious' walk, where rain is likely to affect you, there are ways you can protect yourself from wet weather, but if you're a beginner, just don't go out in the rain. Unless you're sticking to pavements and there's no wind, it's not a good idea to take an umbrella on a walking expedition, however short, because it's not only cumbersome but could be blown inside out by the wind. A hood on your jacket, or a rain hat, is much to be preferred.

As far as muddying your clothes is concerned, it's best in the early days to avoid paths prone to mud, but if that's not possible, pop on some overtrousers or wellies (although wellies aren't to be recommended for walks of more than half a day).

ARE THOSE WEATHER SAYINGS TRUE?

Red sky at night, shepherd's delight – if the cause of the red sky is rays of the setting sun reflected on very high clouds, it means a cold front has passed and settled weather is on the way.

Red sky in the morning, shepherd's warning – if the cause of the red sky is the rays of the morning sun shining on high clouds, it means a warm front is approaching, bringing rain.

Rain before seven, fair before eleven – unless the depression bringing the rain is very deep, evidenced by very thick, fast-moving low-lying clouds, it rarely rains non-stop for more than 4 hours.

Avoid getting too hot or too cold – by wearing appropriate clothing. The best advice here, which is equally valid for more adventurous walking, is to wear thin clothing that you can add to or subtract by extra or fewer layers depending on how hot or cold you are. The layers should be capable of covering the arms and the legs if the sun is hot. In particularly hot sunshine a sun hat is advisable. It may seem counter-intuitive to cover up in hot weather but unprotected skin exposed to hot sun will almost certainly get burnt. Excessive cold is equally unpleasant, if not more so, so add more layers including gloves if necessary, and a woolly hat that will cover the ears. Cold ears can be very uncomfortable! You can always take off outer layers once you've worked up some heat.

Avoid thirst – by taking a bottle of water and drinking from it at frequent regular intervals and not waiting until you're thirsty. Thirst is the consequence of dehydration and by then it's too late. Thirst is a hidden menace – it's impossible to imagine how bad it is until you're experiencing it for yourself, and when you do, you're unable to think of anything else except quenching it. By drinking regularly and frequently from the start, you'll avoid thirst on even the hottest days. This could be supplemented by a hot drink from a thermos. Of course, as well as your trusty water bottle and flask, another tip – and indeed one of the great joys when walking – is to factor in a visit to a pub or cafe where you can refresh yourself with a drink of tea, coffee or something stronger, and a meal or snack. Similarly, you can avoid hunger by taking food with you; you may not need much on a short walk, especially on top of Sunday lunch, but a couple of hours' brisk walking soon builds up an appetite. You may want to invest in a small rucksack to avoid having to carry your food or drink in a bag or a pocket. When you embark on longer walks, it becomes essential that you do have proper supplies of food and drink.

Avoid wearing yourself out – by making sure you aren't over-ambitious. It's a bad idea to walk 5 miles (8 km) from home and then realise your legs and feet are so stiff and achey you can't actually walk home again, especially if you've no way of getting a lift or a bus back to your front door. Start gently, perhaps aiming to do no more than 2 miles (3.2 km), which should take you between 40 minutes and an hour, on your first outing. You can then gradually increase your mileage as your fitness levels improve and your legs and feet get used to it.

Avoid sore feet – next to thirst, aching or blistered feet is the most demoralising experience for a walker. Remember though that blisters or other irritations of the feet are caused not by excessive walking but by inappropriate footwear. If you're still at the beginning of your walking career you don't need a pair of heavy walking boots, but at the other extreme, slippers, slip-ons and flipflops aren't appropriate either, nor is any fashion footwear. A pair of comfortable, stout outdoor shoes or trainers with robust chunky soles, protected by a pair of thick socks or two layers of thin socks, will be fine. Experiment a bit in the early days, deciding what feels comfiest. Just make sure that if you get attached to a particular pair of socks you put them in the wash once in a while!

IN SUMMARY, THEN, IN YOUR EARLY WALKS FOR PLEASURE:

- Choose a fine day
- Clothe yourself sensibly
- Make sure your feet are comfortable
- Don't be overambitious
- Stick to roads, paths and tracks you know – or learn to map read!
- Take a bottle of water and some food

… Now enjoy!

Now you've learnt what it is to be walking for pleasure, you can start to appreciate what's going on around you and what your immediate surroundings have to offer.

'Slow means being present, living each moment fully, putting quality before quantity.'

Carl Honoré, *In Praise of Slow*

PLAY I-SPY...

As mentioned above, one of the great joys of walking is the ability to take things in at a much more leisurely pace than is possible when in the car, bus or train. With walking for pleasure comes the ability to notice so much more, including many features and phenomena you may either have taken for granted and/or never paid any real attention to before.

Look out for some of these on a short walk from home. How many did you know about before? (Note – some may only make seasonal appearances!)

- An old house or cottage (look out for dates sometimes inscribed on the walls), especially one timbered or thatched

- A historic public building, e.g. church or village school

- An unusual or distinctive building, e.g. windmill

- Remains of a prehistoric construction, e.g. earthwork or fort

- A ruin, e.g. of a castle or abbey

- A wild flower or cluster of wild flowers, e.g. buttercup, cowslip, primrose

- A wild rabbit, hare, squirrel, fox or other non-domesticated animal

- Any tree or plant containing wild fruit, e.g. apples, blackberries

- A butterfly with wings of more than one colour

- A bird with distinctive or colourful plumage

- The course of a former railway or canal or remains of a bridge or other paraphernalia associated with it

- An area of water or watercourse, particularly one supporting a variety of fish or other water creatures

- An outcrop of rocks in an otherwise unremarkable landscape

- A wartime construction, e.g. an air-raid shelter or pillbox

- (And very twenty-first century) an old red phone box reused for some other purpose!

Walking is truly an all-the-year-round activity. There's the satisfaction and interest in watching the seasons change, the bare deciduous trees giving way to the lush new green leaves of spring, the abundance of March daffodils, the appearance of apple and cherry blossom and scent of wild garlic in April, the creamy white of hawthorn in May, the profusion of butterflies and insects on a languid summer's afternoon, the abundance of apples in orchards in late August, the profusion of blackberries right across late summer, the golden and reddish hues of autumn, the flurry of autumn leaves cascading from the trees on a windy afternoon in woodland, a sharp frost coating the sun-drenched downland on a December morning, and the snow-capped hillsides of a winter's afternoon.

'Loveliest of trees, the cherry now
Is hung with bloom along the bough,
And stands about the woodland ride
Wearing white for Eastertide.'

A. E. Housman, *A Shropshire Lad*

Q WHAT'S THE BEST AREA IN BRITAIN TO ENJOY WILDLIFE WITH EASY WALKING?

A North Norfolk coast – there's a designated North Norfolk coast path between Hunstanton and Cromer, very easy walking all the way, and in the course of it you might see some, or all, of these birds, animals and insects:

Knot, curlew, dunlin, brent goose, Egyptian goose, starling, finch, skylark, redstart, flycatcher, bearded tit, marsh harrier, godwit, avocet, sandwich tern, little tern, common tern, ringed plover, grey plover, wryneck, wintering twite, snow bunting, shorelark, woodlark, brambling, fieldfare, red-throated diver, teal, wigeon, sanderling, snipe, oystercatcher, dragonfly, common seal and natterjack toad – how many of these did you spot on your Norfolk coast walk?

CREATE THEMED WALKS

You can broaden your appreciation of exploring in your local area by concocting themed walks of your own:

TRY THESE THEMED WALKS

◆ Exploring all public footpaths within a 2-mile (3.2-km) radius of your home

◆ Following all rivers/watercourses within a 2-mile (3.2-km) radius of your home

◆ A walk linking all the pubs or cafes (or both!) in your home town

◆ A walk linking all the places of worship, past or present, in your home town

◆ A walk linking your local railway station with the next station

For many, the best kind of themed walking is wildlife and plant-life walking, wherever you are. Even in the throbbing metropolis that is London you can watch the wildlife and plant life unfold through your walks during the year.

'I have desired to go where springs not fail,
To fields where flies no sharp and sided hail,
And a few lilies blow'

Gerard Manley Hopkins, *'Heaven-Haven'*

A LONDON WILDLIFE YEAR

- A winter's day walk by the Lea Valley Reservoirs with sights of wintering birds such as gadwall, pochard, shoveler, goosander, smew and phalarope

- A spring walk through the daffodils of Lesnes Abbey Woods in Greenwich

- A bluebell walk through Kings Wood in Croydon

- Admiring the April/May flowering of catkins in the hornbeam woods of Epping, Hainault and Ruislip

- A summer afternoon's wander by the Thames watching for mute swan and mallard

- A balmy summer evening's stroll in Belgravia watching for the blackcap, goldfinch or spotted flycatcher, or a promenade in Highgate Cemetery watching for speckled wood butterfly, tawny owl, urban fox, hedgehog, badger or pipistrelle bat

- An autumn walk in one of the royal parks as the leaves change from green to red and gold, watching for heron and cormorant, great crested grebe or Canada goose on the park lakes, or goldcrest, nuthatch, kestrel, woodpigeon, pied wagtail, chaffinch, robin or woodpecker in the trees

- Then back to Lea Valley and the cycle resumes...

SOME TIPS AND HINTS FOR WALKERS SEEKING FLORA AND FAUNA

- *Do* invest in some binoculars – inexpensive, easy to use and may enable you to identify wildlife you might otherwise have missed.

- *Do* make an early start – dawn is a marvellous time to observe wildlife.

- *Don't* take the plant to the book – take the book to the plant – there's no need to pick a plant to name it.

- *Don't* disturb animals or endanger rare plants.

- *Do* beware of scaring birds when they're nesting; species which appear to be tame may simply be reluctant to leave their eggs.

- *Do* watch you don't trample delicate plants when looking for other species.

- *Do* avoid disturbing species in the breeding season.

- *Do* remember that a quiet, careful observer will see more wildlife than a noisy, clumsy one.

'What do we see at once but a little robin! There is no need to burst into tears Fotherington-Thomas swete tho he be.'

Geoffrey Willans and Ronald Searle, *Down with Skool*

THE COUNTRYSIDE CODE – HEADLINE MESSAGES

Whatever walking you do, remember the Countryside Code:

Code for the public
Respect other people
1. Consider the local community and other people enjoying the outdoors.
2. Leave gates and property as you find them and follow paths unless wider access is available.

Protect the natural environment
1. Leave no trace of your visit and take your litter home.
2. Keep dogs under effective control.

Enjoy the outdoors
1. Plan ahead and be prepared.
2. Follow advice and local signs.

Code for land managers
1. Know your rights, responsibilities and liabilities.

> 2. Make it easier for visitors to act responsibly.
> 3. Identify possible threats to visitors' safety.
>
> Fuller explanations of these headline messages are available on the Countryside Code website.

'I never saw daffodils so beautiful – they grew among the mossy stones about and about them – some rested their heads upon these stones as on a pillow for weariness, and the rest tossed and reeled and danced and seemed as if they verily laughed with the wind that blew upon them over the lake.'

Dorothy Wordsworth

GOING FURTHER AFIELD

Congratulations. You've completed your first few local walks. You may be happy with what you're doing, and not want to do any more than enjoy and appreciate your locality and the riches of history, wildlife and scenery it has to offer, perhaps on Sunday afternoon strolls. Many are happy never to do any more and still find joy in their walking.

On the other hand you may be hungry for more. But while you want some more purposeful walking, with more cultural and scenic rewards, you may not feel ready yet for more rugged or remote countryside, nor feel you have the ability to read maps or take compass bearings. The great news is that there are many fantastic and very rewarding walks available to those who may not have the confidence, experience and desire to trek into the moors and the mountains and who would prefer to stick to firm surfaces. We'll look at three examples of these now.

CITY/TOWN WALKS

These really are 'win-win'. You'll be walking along pavements or pedestrian walkways, whether on streets or through parks and gardens, so you won't get muddy; roads and streets will all be signed so with the aid of a street plan you won't get lost; if it starts to rain there will be plenty of opportunities for shelter, and there'll be cafes and pubs to welcome you when you need a cuppa or a bite to eat. The chances are there'll be lots to see within a very short space, and if you do feel you've had enough and you're some way from the finish, you'll almost certainly find there's a bus that can get you back there.

In Britain we are blessed with many fine towns and cities which contain a huge number of really notable features, easily covered during the course of a day's walk – overseas, even more so. The best bet is to head for the town or city's tourist information office. It's likely they will be able to provide, quite possibly free of charge, a map of the town or city centre with places of interest marked on it. Even a town or city that's not on the average tourist's bucket list will be likely to boast an interesting church, museum or park that's teeming with wildlife. Look out also for guided walks. The disadvantage of these is that you'll be travelling at the pace dictated by your guide, but since your guide will by definition be an expert on the ground they are covering, you will get to find out a great deal more about the places of interest that you pass. There are some terrific guided 'theme' walks you can do; for instance, many cities offer ghost walks at night, and guided walks are often laid on during city or town arts festivals.

Below we offer three city walks and a town walk, all in England, to get you started – but there's no magic in the choice of cities/towns or routes and you may feel tempted to detour and devise your own variations on the theme.

THREE CITY WALKS TO TRY

LONDON (approximately 3 miles/5 km) – starting from the **London Eye**, *situated by the* **Jubilee Gardens**, *follow the South Bank of the* **river Thames** *downstream – at weekends and in summer this is a really vibrant area with its many stalls and attractions. Pass Hungerford Bridge and the South Bank concert halls including the* **Royal Festival Hall**, *then pass Waterloo Bridge and the* **National Theatre**. *Next comes the exuberant* **Gabriel's Wharf** *plaza, the* **Oxo Tower**, *which houses modern shops, eateries and offices, and the ornate* **Blackfriars Bridge**. *Go on past the thatched timber-framed reconstruction of the* **Globe Theatre**, *originally built by Shakespeare's company, The Lord Chamberlain's Men, to the* **Tate Modern Art Gallery**, *then cross the Thames by the* **Millennium Bridge**, *which takes you straight up to* **St Paul's Cathedral**. *Begun in 1675, the cathedral, with its famous Whispering Gallery and its huge crypt with tombs of Nelson and Wellington, miraculously escaped destruction in the*

Blitz. Head westwards from the cathedral along Ludgate Hill into Fleet Street, passing **St Bride's Church** *with its so-called 'wedding cake' spire, the* **Royal Courts of Justice,** *and on along the Strand (possibly detouring to the right along Bedford Street to the bustling* **Covent Garden Market,** *for 300 years the chief market for fruit, vegetables and flowers in London; its name was originally* Convent *Garden from an old garden that belonged to the monks of Westminster Abbey). This takes you to* **Trafalgar Square** *and* **Nelson's Column,** *170 ft (52 m) high with an 18 ft-high (5-m) statue of Nelson on top of it. Exit Trafalgar Square along Whitehall, passing* **Horse Guards Parade, Downing Street** *– the official residence of the Prime Minister since 1732 – the early seventeenth-century* **Banqueting House** *(the first example in England of the new Classical style of architecture, introduced from Italy) and the* **Cenotaph,** *reaching Parliament Square, on the far side of which is* **Westminster Abbey,** *described as the most beautiful Gothic church in London. Turn eastwards from Parliament Square to pass the* **Houses of Parliament** *and* **Big Ben;** *Big Ben isn't the bell tower but the actual bell, named after the First Commissioner of Works, Sir Benjamin Hall (the tower contains cells where MPs can be imprisoned for breach of parliamentary privilege) and cross* **Westminster Bridge,** *bearing left onto the riverbank past the huge old County Hall building to return to the London Eye.*

BATH *(approximately 2 miles/3.2 km) – from the station walk north up Manvers Street into Pierrepont Street, passing Parade Gardens and reaching the covered* **Pulteney Bridge,** *completed in 1773 and named after William Pulteney, reputedly the wealthiest man in Britain at that time. Bear left here into Bridge Street, shortly bearing right into Northgate Street and then left into Broad Street; at the end bear left into George Street then right into Gay Street, bringing you to the eighteenth-century* **Circus,** *off which is Bennett Street with its* **Museum of East Asian Art** *and* **Fashion Museum.** *Head westwards along Brock Street to reach* **Royal Crescent** *with its magnificent Regency architecture, the work of John Wood the Younger, between 1767 and 1774. Retrace your steps via the Circus and Gay Street, going straight on this time, perhaps visiting the* **Jane Austen Centre,** *then continuing past Queen Square into Barton Street, bearing round left into Westgate Street and forward into Cheap Street. Detour to the right to reach the square containing* **Bath Abbey** *(founded in 1499 by Bishop of Bath, Oliver King), the eighteenth-century* **Pump Room,** *and* **Roman Baths.** *These are among the best-preserved Roman remains anywhere in England, dating back almost 2,000 years, although the waters themselves, supposed to have healing qualities, were described in Dickens'* Pickwick Papers *as tasting like 'warm flat-irons'. Pick up York Street on the south side of the Pump Room, following it eastwards past* **Sally Lunn's House,** *one of the oldest houses in Bath with Roman and medieval foundations, named after a Huguenot refugee (her name was anglicised) who created a rich round bread named the Sally Lunn Bun. You arrive at Pierrepont Street, turning right to retrace your steps to the station.*

YORK *(approximately 2 miles/3.2 km) – from the station turn left into Station Road, soon passing Leeman Road with the* **National Railway Museum,** *which boasts over a hundred locomotives including one of the earliest,* Puffing Billy, *and the world's fastest steam locomotive, the* Mallard. *Go round to the right, turning left at the crossroads and crossing* **Lendal Bridge,** *continuing past* **Lendal Tower** *and along Museum Street, with Museum Gardens to the left housing the* **Yorkshire Museum.** *Bear left round into St Leonard's Place and right into High Petergate, going forward into Minster Yard and Deangate, immediately adjoining* **York Minster,** *which was built between 1220 and 1472 and has magnificent medieval stained-glass windows. Fork left to detour into the Minster precinct to visit* **St William's College** *in College Street, and, a bit further on, the seventeenth-century* **Treasurer's House,** *where ghosts of a Roman legion are still reputed to march through the cellars. Return to Deangate and follow it to Bedern Hall, turning right into Goodramgate, bearing left at the end and going straight on down the* **Shambles,** *a street of timber-framed cottages where at one time there were twenty-six butchers' shops – or'shambles' (derived from the word 'shamel', a shelf below a butcher's window where meat was sold). You arrive at Pavement and turn right to follow it. Go forward into Coppergate past the* **Jorvik Viking Centre,** *a reconstruction of the sights, sounds and even smells of Viking York, built on the site where Viking remains were first discovered. Bear left into Clifford Street going forward into Tower Street, detouring off Clifford Street to visit the* **York Dungeon** *and off Tower Street to visit the* **Regimental Museum** *and* **Clifford's Tower,** *the keep from the old castle, founded* *in 1068 and rebuilt in the thirteenth century. Just beyond is the **York Castle Museum**, which boasts a life-size replica of a Victorian street and the original cell where Dick Turpin was held. At the end of Tower Street turn right, crossing Skeldergate Bridge into Bishopgate Street, soon turning right to join the **city wall**. The walls were built on Roman foundations and date from the twelfth century. Follow the wall clockwise, parallel with Nunnery Lane and Queen Street, to return to the station.*

And here's an English town walk to try:

*RYE, EAST SUSSEX (approximately 1.5 miles/2.4 km) From the station exit make your way straight up Station Approach, over Cinque Ports Street and up Market Road, turning right into the High Street, which swings to the left and becomes the Mint. At the junction of the Mint and Mermaid Street turn right and walk down towards the waterfront, shortly reaching the **Rye Heritage Centre**, which is immediately to your right; it includes an amazing depiction of how Rye was in 1872 with lighting and commentary. Cross over the main road, South Undercliff, and bear right, then shortly left round a barrier to access the **quay**, turning left to follow the waterfront downstream. At the exit, by the left bend of the road, leave the quay and cross the road, going over into **Strand**, with its restored black-painted wooden warehouses, following it to arrive back at the bottom of cobbled **Mermaid Street**. Now turn right to follow it uphill, passing the timber-framed early sixteenth-century **Mermaid Inn**, and at the top turn right into West Street, shortly reaching the eighteenth-century redbrick **Lamb House**, which is to your right. It is best* known for its association with the novelists E. F. Benson and Henry James, who both lived here, Benson being the author of the Mapp & Lucia books, set in and around Rye. Follow West Street to **Church Square** and turn immediately right to reach the top end of **Watchbell Street**, turning right again to walk down this beautiful street and enjoy an excellent view from its bottom end by the **Hope Anchor Inn**. Follow Watchbell Street back to Church Square and go straight on to the far (northeastern) end, bearing right to reach **Ypres Tower**. Built in 1249, it's one of Rye's oldest buildings, built as the castle of Rye but subsequently becoming a prison. There's a museum within the tower, and beyond it in **Gun Garden** there's a platform with a display of cannons and cannonballs, and excellent views towards the sea. Now walk along the east side of the square to a T-junction with **Market Street**, turning right and walking past the fifteenth-century timber-framed **Flushing Inn**. Veer left down East Street, passing **Rye Castle Museum** on the left; this includes a wide range of attractions, from a 1745 fire engine to a Captain Pugwash treasure hunt (John Ryan, writer of the Pugwash books, made his home in Rye). At the end, turn right into the **High Street** and follow it briefly as far as the **telescope** and a **splendid viewpoint**, continuing along the street to reach the fourteenth-century **Landgate**, the last remaining one of Rye's original medieval gates. Walk back along the High Street until you come to **Lion Street,** which is to the left, while to your right here is the **Old Grammar School** with its distinctive Dutch gables, dating back to 1636. Turn left by the **George Inn** up Lion Street, now heading for the church; on the right, just before you reach the church, is **Simon the Pieman tearoom** *and the fifteenth-century timber-framed **Fletcher's House**, the birthplace of the dramatist John Fletcher in 1579, while to the left, pretty much opposite the tearoom, is the fine arcaded eighteenth-century **Town Hall**. The **Norman church of St Mary**, immediately beyond, is famous for its sixteenth-century clock, the oldest working church turret clock in the country. Turn right (as you look towards the church entrance) immediately before the church along a pedestrian passage past the pink-painted **Old Vicarage** and some cottages with lovely gardens, arriving back at West Street; follow it back to Lamb House, veering right and walking back to the High Street. Turn right to follow it to the junction with Lion Street, crossing over and now doubling back along the south side of the High Street. Shortly turn right into Market Road and walk straight on from there to the station.*

NINE CITIES AROUND THE WORLD TO SAVOUR – ON FOOT

NEW YORK – New York is so easy for the walker with its numbered streets and avenues; you can never really get lost and if walking from A to B can monitor your progress very easily. For the independent traveller, what could beat a straight walk from Central Park with its Strawberry Fields, all the way down through Manhattan via Times Square and Wall Street to Battery Park at its very southern tip, with views to the Statue of Liberty across the water. If you're in a hurry you can do it easily enough in a couple of hours but with its shops, museums and architecture, from the Flatiron building to the daddy of them all, the Empire State, it may take you a week! In 2017 Explore was offering a bespoke seven-day walking tour: it begins in the heart of Manhattan, stopping at Fifth Avenue, Little Italy and Times Square, then wandering the streets of Harlem, capital of African-American culture and incorporating attendance at a Gospel Mass; the journey then roams Central Park with its intriguing mix of buildings and vegetation, before heading to DUMBO, a former manufacturing district in Brooklyn turned into a neighbourhood lined with artists' studios, workshops and boutiques; then it takes a jaunt through Greenwich Village, and a stroll along the High Line, a park built on a freight rail line elevated above Manhattan's West Side; and finally, it ends at the Railyards with views of the city and Hudson River.

TOKYO – Given the vastness and busyness of the city you might find a walk around Japan's capital quite daunting. But it can be done. Walk Japan have conceived a two-day itinerary exploring the city's history from its feudal Samurai past to the present. On Day 1 you're given glimpses into the lives of the shoguns (military dictators), daimyo (feudal lords) and samurai warriors of pre-modern Japan, while on Day 2 you're provided with an insight into the lives of the townspeople of the Edo period. Highlights include a visit to Koishikawa Korakuen, one of the oldest parks in the city, a trip to the Edo-Tokyo museum, the site of Edo Castle, which is now the Imperial Palace, and the neighbourhood of Yanaka with its lanes, quaint houses and traditional shops.

LISBON – The westernmost city in Europe was largely destroyed by the 1755 earthquake but substantial parts of the city were left standing. The principal sights of modern Lisbon are concentrated into a relatively small area and are easily accessible on foot. That said, because Lisbon is constructed on a series of hills, be prepared for some up-and-down work! The heart of the city is the Rossio/Baixa area, with its swish shopping streets and huge squares at either end, but by heading eastwards from this area the walker will soon reach the Sé (cathedral) and enter the area of Lisbon known as Alfama with its seemingly endless network of cobbled streets and alleys, reaching their climax at the hilltop castle ruin. From here there is a quite unforgettable panorama of the city and the estuary of the River Tagus beside which the city is built. Beyond the castle a walk on through Alfama brings you to lookouts known as *miradouros*, with similarly fantastic views of the city, the river and the countryside beyond. A short train ride takes the walker to Belém, with its magnificent suspension bridge over the river, a cluster of fascinating historic buildings and museums, and a splendid waterfront walk linking a monument to early voyages of discovery with the extraordinarily photogenic Belém Tower on the shore.

PARIS – This most romantic of cities lends itself to walking and enjoying. Starting from the Gare du Nord, it's not far to the Ile de la Cité to admire Notre Dame, the Palais de Justice and the Hôtel de Ville; from there head via the spectacular Opera House to the Place de Palais Royal with its shops, gardens and truly palatial buildings. Walk on to the Louvre, into the Tuileries and down to the Place de la Concorde with its breathtaking views to the Arc de Triomphe and Eiffel Tower, reached in turn by way of the Champs-Élysées (Elysian Fields). Returning to the main shopping area, cheat a little by using the funicular railway to reach the Sacré-Coeur basilica and Montmartre, with its magnificent (and unlike the Eiffel Tower, free to enjoy) views over the city. Throw in food and wine, and you have the perfect city walk which you could cram into a single day or spread over a week or more. There are plenty of bespoke tours available of Paris, including food tours, to cater for all tastes.

BELFAST – Though this would have been completely off limits in the 1970s, when the Troubles were at their height, this is a fascinating city to explore on foot, contrasting the regeneration of the city from those dark times with the relics and reminders of the city's violent past. While it doesn't make for comfortable walking at times, and the closely packed terraces and divides between them generate a tension of their own, you can create your own reliving of the Troubles by walking up Falls Road, Shankill Road and Crumlin Road, passing the many murals on the sides of housing terraces, and stopping at the Crumlin Gaol, where so many political prisoners and internees were housed. But within easy walking distance of the main shopping area, on the eastern side of the city, is the Titanic exhibition, offering a fascinating and absorbing insight into the genesis and construction of this most infamous of ocean liners. Then a short bus ride from the centre offers the possibility of a walk up Cave Hill, from where there is a superb view across the whole city and beyond.

VENICE – The only ways round Venice are by boat or on foot, and one of the great joys of Venice is exploring the countless waterside paths and alleys away from the tourist honeypots of St Mark's Square and the Canal Grande. The city is made up of over a hundred different islands, each one containing a number of narrow walkways dotted with little shops, restaurants, churches and historic brick buildings with often ornate balconies, each island linked to its neighbour by one or more bridges. There's seldom a dead end, but half the fun of an island-hop is not knowing where the walkway will take you – if anywhere! If you do reach a dead end and find yourself gazing at another stretch of water, who knows, you could be entertained and even serenaded by a passing gondolier. And simply the walk around St Mark's Square with its cathedral, colonnaded Doge's Palace, Campanile and exclusive shops, could take you all day. It's possible to take a seven-day art history tour, all on foot, through the city, visiting such gems as San Zaccaria and San Giovanni in Bragora, and churches with Renaissance altarpieces by such greats as Vivarini and Bellini.

KRAKOW – This isn't the largest city in Poland but it has an astonishing combination of fantastic architecture and walking possibilities that put you in touch with an important and immensely poignant aspect of the city's past. You might spend a whole day walking round the environs of the central square, Rynek Główny, dominated by its basilica of St Mary, Cloth Hall and town hall tower offering astonishing city views; a shortish walk from here takes you to the Wawel area of the city, an ensemble of buildings perched on a 165-ft (50-m) rock at the southern end of the old town including the cathedral and castle, and mementoes of Pope John Paul II, who enjoys almost iconic status in the city. The poignancy comes as you enter the Jewish quarter of the city, Kazimierz, and replicate the walk taken during the Holocaust by Jews from here to a ghetto area across the river; a museum, housed in the old 'Under The Eagle' pharmacy, is devoted to ghetto life. You can continue the walk to Płaszów, a labour camp beyond the ghetto, where thousands of Krakow's Jews perished at the hands of the Nazis, and could then return to the city centre via the Schindler Museum, devoted to the work of a man who during the Holocaust saved hundreds of Jews from certain death. In many ways this is a more rewarding walk than a visit to nearby Auschwitz, which has arguably become too commercialised and crowded with visitors.

EDINBURGH – The capital of Scotland offers walks for every season. May is the best time of year to visit the Georgian New Town and the Royal Botanic Garden, where the colours of the plants and shrubs will be at their most dazzling. In August the Edinburgh Festival and Military Tattoo may draw you to the Royal Mile, where you could spend all day on a walk up this street of sumptuous architecture, starting with Holyrood House, the palace of Scottish monarchs in the sixteenth and seventeenth centuries, culminating in the remarkable Camera Obscura and then Edinburgh Castle with its crown and sceptre of the kings and queens of Scotland; then you could head for one of the many Festival fringe attractions that are dotted all over the city. November or December may see you drawn to the shops on

Princes Street. It is just a 25-minute climb from the city centre to the summit of the extraordinary Arthur's Seat crag, from which on a clear day you can enjoy a complete panorama of the whole city, the Pentland Hills, the Southern Uplands and the Firth of Forth with its magnificent bridge crossings.

CAPE TOWN – In Cape Town, South Africa's legislative capital, you as walker have the best of both worlds – city and countryside. Walking through the city streets, perhaps on one of the walking tours on offer, may bring you to Greenmarket Square, where slaves were once sold; City Hall, where Nelson Mandela made his first speech as a free man; Auwal Masjid, the oldest mosque in South Africa; and the so-called Bo-Kaap Walk, with brightly coloured houses of pink, green, blue and orange. Then you can leave the city centre behind you, a 2- to 3-hour walk taking you via the Platteklip Gorge to the summit of Cape Town's most iconic landmark, Table Mountain, 3,562 ft (1,086 m) high. Having enjoyed the superb views to the city and the South Atlantic you could return by cable car. A more leisurely walk in the city's vicinity is along the Green Point promenade, which may provide sightings of seals, dolphins and whales.

'I wandered lonely as a cloud that floats on high o'er vales and hills.'

William Wordsworth

OLD RAILWAY WALKS

Early in the twentieth century, Britain enjoyed a very extensive network of country railways. However, many proved to be uneconomical to run and as a result, under the notorious British Rail chairman Dr Beeching, vast numbers of rural railway lines were closed. Some were revived as preserved steam railways; some were left to their fate and were built on; but some have been turned into walkways for pedestrian and cycle use.

By definition they provide very easy walking: a firm surface, little or no climbing, and no navigational difficulties. And they have the advantage over city or town walks of being more peaceful, many passing through very beautiful countryside, including farmland, woodland and rolling hill country. There is one catch – their starts and finishes aren't always easily accessible by public transport.

Try these (or parts of these!). They're all superb examples of this type of walking at its best.

Monsal Trail, Derbyshire – An 8.5-mile (13.5-km) walk from Blackwell Mill in Chee Dale, near Buxton, to Coombs Road at Bakewell, through beautiful Peak District countryside and with the added interest of four tunnels, each about 400 yds long, and two shorter tunnels.

Mawddach Trail, Gwynedd – A 9.5-mile (15-km) walk from Dolgellau to Barmouth in North Wales, following the southern edge of the Mawddach Estuary with great views towards Snowdonia.

Downs Link – a 37-mile (59-km) walk from Shoreham-by-Sea in West Sussex to St Martha's just outside Guildford in Surrey. This incorporates a walk along two old railway lines and passes the attractive towns of Steyning and Cranleigh. As its name suggests, the Downs Link does link the South and North Downs escarpments, with lovely views to both.

Rowrah Sculpture Trail, Cumbria – An 11.5-mile (18.5-km) walk from Whitehaven to Rowrah in Cumbria via Cleator Moor, noted for its sculptures reflecting the industrial heritage of the area, with views towards the Lakeland mountains.

Bristol and Bath Railway Path, Somerset – A 13-mile (21-km) walk between these two cities, close to the delightful River Avon and an important wildlife corridor. The restored Bitton station, sculptures at Warmley and a tunnel on the outskirts of Bristol are the highlights.

Craigellachie to Blacksboat section of the Speyside Way in Scotland – Although this is part of a much longer route of 80 miles (128 km), the walk from Craigellachie to Blacksboat is just 10 miles (16 km) and follows the course of the old Speyside Railway. There's an unbeatable combination of the proximity of the magnificent River Spey itself, a fine backcloth of hills and mountains, beautifully kept station buildings, and, for whisky fans, some distilleries!

CANALSIDE WALKS

Canal usage declined with the coming of the railways, but in recent years many of Britain's canals have been restored for leisure use and there are some excellent walks available on canal towpaths, providing easy, level walking through often very beautiful countryside. Navigation will certainly not be a problem as you'll have the canal beside you all the time.

Try these canal walks in full or in part:

Regent's Canal, London – An 8.5-mile (13.5-km) walk from Little Venice to Limehouse in London, taking you through sections of the capital that you may well never have explored, including Camden Town, Islington, De Beauvoir Town, Haggerston, Victoria Park and Mile End – where North London meets East London.

Leeds and Liverpool Canal – A 16-mile (25.5-km) walk along the Aire Valley towpath section between Leeds and Bingley, incorporating townscapes, lovely West Yorkshire countryside and some historic sites.

Caledonian Canal – The section of Great Glen Way between Banavie, near Fort William on the west coast of Scotland, and Fort Augustus is some 28 miles (45 km) and follows sections of the Caledonian Canal interspersed with Lochs Lochy and Oich – very easy walking with superb mountain views, including Ben Nevis.

Montgomeryshire and Brecon Canal – this section of towpath of just over 30 miles (48 km) begins at Brecon and ends at Cwmbran in south Wales; described as one of the most picturesque in the UK, it provides stunning views of mountains, most notably the Brecon Beacons, as well as lovely walking through river valleys and woodland. The towpath is in excellent condition with easy access to good pubs.

Grantham Canal – This walk along the Grantham Canal towpath through the Vale of Belvoir in Nottinghamshire stretches for 33 miles (53 km) between Grantham and Nottingham and includes Cotgrave Country Park, with a heron lake, woodland, wetland and grassland.

The Thames Path – Arguably the ultimate inland waterside walk in Britain, it follows the River Thames for most of its length, has excellent firm surfaces and navigation really couldn't be easier. But it's still a challenge for the walker, being 185 miles (296 km) long. Try it a bit at a time, perhaps using the book *From Source to Sea* by Tom Chesshyre, which details his walk along the entire route.

ORGANISED WALKS/WALKING CLUBS

If by now you want to be even more ambitious in your walking but still don't have the confidence to tackle more demanding routes either on your own, or with your companions, you could join a walking organisation.

The biggest walking organisation by far is the Ramblers. With your membership you will receive their quarterly *WALK* magazine, with lots of described walks of varying degrees of difficulty plus plenty of articles about walking generally, advice on equipment etc, and you'll get details of the thousands of organised and guided walks that take place throughout the year. But there are many other ramblers' clubs as well, offering guided/group walks on which you're sure to increase your confidence as a walker, and possibly make some new friends along the way. You can access details of your local ones online or in your local public library. In addition, check out your local paper or community magazine/newsletter for lists of guided walks in your neighbourhood, for which you can just turn up without having to be a member of a group.

If you prefer your 'more ambitious' walks in small doses but don't necessarily want to commit to an organisation, you could undertake a one-off programme of guided walks in a specific locality over a limited period of time. A great way of facilitating this is through walking festivals. What makes walking festivals so special is firstly the enormous range of walks on offer, with something to suit every taste, but also the opportunity to meet other walkers and make lasting friendships. The presence of other walkers and guides to assist you ensures your walking will be safe and pleasurable but still potentially challenging and exciting. Après-walk activities may include not only dinners and barbecues but lectures and workshops. Some countries have embraced the concept; others are lagging behind rather!

These are examples of walking festivals around the world that have been held in 2017 and are likely to be repeated at least once every two years. Full details of these are available on the internet.

Scilly Isles Walking Festival – the Festival, held in early April, comprised 29 walks spread across Scilly's five inhabited islands and three uninhabited ones. It was possible to explore a different island each day, and enjoy cross-island walks. Expert guides led themed walks covering everything from foraging and wildlife spotting to maritime history.

Mourne International Walking Festival – the Festival, held in June, was centred on the Mountains of Mourne in County Down, Northern Ireland. The Festival brought together an excellent range of walks suitable for all levels of fitness and ability with routes at both high and low level, from a 6-mile (10-km) road/track walk to a 12.5-mile (20-km) guided mountain hike. Après-walk activities included a Blister Ball!

Tenerife Walking Festival – the Festival, held in May, was an open event for hikers from all over the world, combining different types of hikes and trails, including five coastal hikes, 12 volcanic hikes and five forest hikes. There were also numerous après-walk activities including lectures, a workshop on nature photography, and intriguingly, 'gastronomic space and nature'.

Canberra Walking Festival – the Festival is an annual event, held in late March or early April, and centres on the capital city of Australia. Walkers can choose their own walking challenge, from 3 miles (5 km) to a full marathon, and there is a huge range of walks available reflecting the tremendously varied scenery on the fringes of the city, including the iconic Lake Burley Griffin, nature reserves and areas of bush and forest.

Rotorua Walking Festival – the Festival is held each March. It's one of a number in New Zealand; other festivals are based at Waiheke and Manawatu. Day 1 at Rotorua includes walks in the majestic Whakarewarewa Forest, with distances of between 6 miles (10 km), 13 miles (21 km) and 26 miles (42 km) to choose from, while Day 2 provides the opportunity to visit hot thermal springs, bubbling mud pools, lakes and majestic redwoods.

Cape Garden Route Festival – advertised as taking place every Easter, this Festival, currently the only one in South Africa, is based in the Western Cape area, centring on Sedgefield and Plettenberg in the area between the Outeniqua Mountains and Plettenberg Bay. There are more than 52 walks available, scattered over a wide area, over the Easter weekend.

Rogue Valley Riches – this Festival, held in May, is a biennial event in southern Oregon, USA. It explores the beautiful trails in the Lost Creek Lake area, where there is a magnificent meeting of wide, fast-flowing water and thick forest. There's a choice of six walking routes, ranging from easy to challenging, with dam, ridge and gorge exploration among others, and there's a wide range of social activity advertised too.

Victoria Volkssport Phoenix Festival – this Festival, held in Victoria, British Columbia, the so-called 'City of Gardens' and also known as the Vacation Capital of Canada, takes place every other year and offers a huge range of walks across a long weekend ranging from 3-mile (5-km) walks to marathons. As well as city walks there are also lakeside and forest trails and walks with ocean and mountain views. Again, there are ample après-walk activities, including a Saturday evening festival dinner.

And now you're ready for a walk on the wild side...

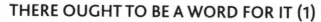

THERE OUGHT TO BE A WORD FOR IT (1)

Feeling of utter bliss at removing your walking boots during mid-walk break

Disappointment on discovering bus needed to access proposed walk is limited to one every Monday morning excluding bank holidays

Amazement on discovering that people you meet on a walk absolutely miles from nowhere and at least 300 miles from home live two streets away from you

Reluctance to bare arms or legs during hot day's walk for fear of exposing embarrassing tattoos you drunkenly had done in Southend two years ago

Sense of guilt you feel deserting your partner and four children for a walking holiday, however well-earned, leading to over-solicitous phone call on first night away, presentation of over-generous gifts on return, and rash promise to take them all on a beach holiday somewhere intolerably hot and expensive

Reaching what you believe is the top of the hill only to see another, much steeper hillside rising up behind it

Stage of challenging walk where your guide or internet notes tell you, 'This is where most walkers who are going to give up, do so'

Pleasing smell of newly unpacked expensive walking jacket, fresh from its cellophane wrapping

Heavy mid-walk meal, much enjoyed at the time, which then weighs so heavily on your stomach as you set off again that you wish you'd just stuck to the salad bar

Unspecified location in a distant galaxy, to which the single unused bootlace from a new pair of boots disappears, never to be traced when needed at a later date

4 | WILDER WALKING

> *'On the top there are no signposts,*
> *no markers. Only the choice of channels*
> *between the chocolate-covered peat.'*

John Hillaby, *Journey Through Britain*

You've enjoyed a potter in Bath, or a stroll by the Regent's Canal, or pretending to be a steam train puffing through the Peak District. And maybe it's the sight of all those hills in the Peak District or the hills rising up behind the Caledonian Canal that now makes you want to head for the hills and to tackle some of the wilder, more remote and mountainous countryside of Great Britain.

The good news – the rewards in terms of the scenery, the views and the greater variety of plant life and wildlife are massive. There is the enticing prospect of mountains soaring to 4,000 ft (1,200 m), ridgetops and clifftops looking out across whole counties, sightings of golden eagle, osprey and puffin.

The less good news – you need to be much better prepared. All the ground rules set out in the above chapters apply, but there are many more things you need to be aware of if your walk is to be a joy, and not a disaster.

Now it gets serious.

WILDER WALKING Q & A 1

Q What do we mean by wilder walking?
A In this chapter we mean:
Hills and fells
Forests
Clifftops
Moorland
Mountains (Note – in this book we do not cover mountaineering but confine ourselves to ascents of mountains that can be managed with ordinary walking gear and without specialist mountain equipment such as ice axes, ropes, crampons, etc.)

WILDER WALKING Q & A 2

Q What are the risks of wilder walking?
A The walking is more strenuous – you need stamina.
The terrain is tougher underfoot – you need decent footwear.

> The weather will be unpredictable – you need decent clothing.
>
> There will be fewer landmarks – you need to be able to map read and know where you are.
>
> There'll be fewer amenities – you need to bring food and drink.
>
> You may get into difficulties – you need to take precautions.
>
> You may have a lot to carry – you need a good rucksack.

ABOUT STAMINA

It's a bad idea for your first walk, after years of not-so-blissful indolence, to be a 10-mile (16-km) mountain hike. It's likely to end in tears. If you're a beginner you should follow all the steps and guidance given in Chapter 3, doing lots of walking around your local area, building up your stamina levels until you're sure you can cope with more demanding walking. If your walking has been confined to level countryside, begin to factor in some gentle hill climbing as well. You can practise in everyday life as well, using stairs instead of escalators or lifts. Then, as your confidence and stamina levels increase, you should go in for some more energetic hill climbing. There are plenty of easy and straightforward hill walks you can do, requiring no navigational skills, but choose a fine day for them!

It's important to cultivate good techniques for coping with steep ascents and descents in order to preserve stamina and fitness.

TOP FIVE TIPS FOR HILL WALKING

◆ Shorten your stride when ascending but move your legs at the same speed.

◆ Consider zigzagging on very steep hills – it makes the route longer but less arduous.

◆ Put the whole of the sole of the foot down on firm ground – avoid toe and heel holds.

◆ Don't be tempted to climb your first hill of the day too quickly.

◆ When descending steeply, allow the legs to bend slightly at the knee to avoid jarring the body.

Diet is important as well when embarking on more or longer walks than you are used to. Your ability to cope with wilder walking will be affected if either you're not eating enough, or if you're badly overweight. You also need to ensure you eat properly before you set off. The best sorts of food to include in your meals are those that fill you up but which release energy slowly into the body. Chat to your GP if you want more specific advice.

Always... have a good breakfast before setting off for the day.

Always... stop and eat something if you feel hungry. Your stamina levels will diminish frighteningly quickly if you've an empty stomach.

Always... ensure you have some rest times built into a day's walk to revive yourself.

> **Top tip:** When you stop to rest, choose a spot out of the wind, remove your boots as well as your backpack, and after you've had something to eat and drink lie flat on your back and relax completely – this will help re-energise you both physically and mentally.

Lastly, you mustn't try to do any more miles in a day than you know you're capable of.

NAISMITH'S FORMULA

Naismith's Formula may help: Allow one hour for every 3 miles (5 km) measured on a map plus an additional hour for every 2,000 ft (610 m) climbed. (Note: your walk may not include any single climbs of 2,000 ft but there may be cumulative ascent which far exceeds this.)

Bear in mind that in poor conditions your pace may be significantly slower.

In practice it's better to aim to do a little less than you think you're capable of. That way you can build in time to enjoy the surroundings, and have the occasional rest.

Q WHAT'S THE BEST AREA IN BRITAIN TO WALK FOR SPECTACULAR WILDLIFE FINDS?

A The Cairngorms in northeast Scotland
See in the Cairngorms:

- Osprey on rivers and lochs (there's an observation hide at Loch Garten near Aviemore)
- Golden eagle in the mountains
- Ptarmigan in the mountains
- Dotterel in the mountains
- Peregrine in the mountains
- Buzzard on moorland edges near woodland
- Merlin on the moors
- Red grouse on the moors
- Ring ouzel on the moors
- Snow bunting on the mountains
- Capercaillie in the forests
- Goldeneye around woodland lochs
- Reindeer on the mountains
- Red deer on the moors
- Red squirrel in the forests
- Wildcat in the forests
- Fox in the forests
- Badger in the forests
- Otter in the forests

ABOUT DECENT FOOTWEAR

While trainers or stout outdoor shoes will be fine for level tramping, and for short straightforward hill walks on firm surfaces, these are not sufficient when walking in wilder country.

The following are hazards you may meet underfoot:

- Clay soil – huge lumps can cling to the soles of your footwear
- Wet grass – can be very slippery on inclines
- Mud
- Loose stones/boulders – particularly on hillsides
- Rock covered with slime or lichen
- Peat bogs – a hazard on moorland
- Water – puddles, streams, even rivers which may need to be forded
- Snow and ice in winter

Just a handful of walks in which you encounter such hazards could tear your trainers to shreds.

You need proper walking shoes or boots which won't let in water, which can stand up to the punishment the above hazards may give, and which will be comfortable.

There is a formidable choice out there and it's difficult to know where to start.

Like everything in life, you get what you pay for. It's up to you whether you splash out on a hi-tech, ultra-durable pair for several hundred pounds from a specialist walking goods retailer but which last you forever, or whether you choose the cheapest pair on eBay, in a car boot sale or discount store and find yourself having to replace them after six months. If you're serious about walking, but haven't got unlimited funds, you may want to go somewhere down the middle.

TOP BOOT TIPS

It's vital that you:

- Get decent socks to go with them – loop-stitch socks are recommended – and wearing two pairs means you get extra cushioning for the feet.

- Try the boots on first (taking your walking socks with you), before committing yourself to buying. There should be enough room to poke a forefinger behind the heel and the toes should just touch the boot at the front. They must be 100 per cent comfortable. If they aren't, reject them. If they were ordered online and aren't comfortable, send them back. (In view of the hassle involved with this, boots are better purchased in shops rather than online.)

- Break them in – meaning wear them around the house and for short easy walks before taking them out on a longer tougher walk. Breaking-in helps make them conform to the shape of the feet.

- Clean them after each walk and apply dubbin (or equivalent) for protecting the fabric. Your boot retailer can advise of available products and how to apply them.

Did you know that when walking the coastline of Britain, John Merrill got through three pairs of boots – each of which had been broken in over 500 miles (800 km) first. He changed out of his first pair after wearing them to destruction – they'd done 3,800 miles (6,080 km)!

ABOUT DECENT CLOTHING

The big difference when out wilder walking is that the weather is likely to be much more unpredictable. The chances are you'll do a lot of your wilder walking when on holiday and unless you're very fortunate, some rain will be inevitable, particularly in the Lake District or in western Scotland; generally the weather will be cooler in these regions as well. What you put on must be able to stand up to the worst weather. It could literally be a life-saver.

In colder, wetter weather, it's vitally important that you wear sufficient clothes to keep warm, and that the clothes you wear remain dry and free from moisture and sweat. Several thin layers on top is better than one piece of clothing, whatever kind of walking you do. The most important thing to get right, in terms of clothing, is the jacket.

Any jacket you wear for your wild walking needs to be *waterproof* and *breathable*. A breathable garment lets air in and lets sweat out. Ideally it should contain what's called a wicking fabric. Unlike, say, cotton, which will absorb water and hang onto your sweat – making your clothing, and you, wet and unpleasantly clammy – a wicking fabric, such as polyester, picks up moisture and carries it away from your body, spreading it out to evaporate easily on the outside of the fabric so you stay cool and dry. It's also suggested that your base layer should be a shirt of synthetic material which will wick moisture from the body and reduce chilling.

Top tip: Before embarking on serious walking, seek advice on boots and clothing from a specialist outdoor retailer. Shop around for best value for money but remember you get what you pay for.

ABOUT MAP READING/KNOWING WHERE YOU ARE

Unless you know the terrain very well, it is folly to set out on any unguided walk in countryside you don't know without a map, either a paper map or a screen map using apps such as ifootpath. You cannot rely on signposting alone; it only takes one damaged or non-existent signpost at a path junction to render you completely lost. If conditions are poor, the consequences could be serious.

The choice of paper maps is bewildering, but for the walker in Great Britain by far and away the best is the orange-covered Ordnance Survey (OS) Explorer series. They cover the whole of Great Britain at a scale of 1:25,000 (roughly 2.5 inches to a mile or 4 cm to 1 km) and, given the amount of detail on them, they are astonishingly good value for money.

The Explorer maps show, among many other things:

- All footpaths, bridleways and byways in England and Wales to which the public have access, either unrestricted or permissive

- Field boundaries

- Contours showing relative height

- Access land

- Places of particular scenic or historic interest or importance

- Lines marking the National Grid (meaning that if you select any landmark on the map, you can determine its location as a 'grid reference'. (Instructions on how to ascertain a grid reference are given on each map key).

- It is not only a good idea but essential, having decided on a wild walk, to trace it on a map, in conjunction with the key provided with each map.

- Tracing your route will make you aware of:

- Availability of rights of way/access land for the walk you want to do

- Hazards close to or on your chosen route

- Landmarks which will help you navigate

- Distance and, using Naismith's formula (see p. 82), how long it'll take you

Of course nowadays you may not need a paper map at all; thanks to the internet, it's possible to use the Google Map facility and apps such as ifootpath to provide not only maps on your computer or smartphone screen but an aerial view as well. So you can rehearse the walk before setting out, and relive it afterwards.

When conditions are clear and the path is well defined, you can confidently navigate with a map alone, whether paper or electronic. However you may be caught in mist or fog, particularly on higher ground, and lose all sense of direction. When this happens, you'll need a compass or the use of GPS (either a dedicated GPS device or a navigation app) to get you out of trouble.

The compass is the low-tech option, tried and tested over centuries, not reliant on batteries or signals. It is also harder to use! There are different kinds of compass, and to find out how to use yours, either refer to the instructions accompanying it or go online – or both.

GPS (Global Positioning System) is a network of earth-orbiting satellites that beam signals to earth. The system enables you to determine your position and desired direction of travel at the touch of a few buttons. GPS is reliant on your obtaining a signal, the accuracy of the reading may be compromised by large areas of water or thick tree cover, and it'll be no help at all if your device isn't charged. But if it works as it should it's much easier than taking a compass bearing; it's very reliable and much less fiddly. With the availability of GPS and navigation apps on your own particular technology, it's never been easier for you to navigate yourself through your wild walks. Just remember to charge your battery before setting out. Note that most smartphones and map apps nowadays let you download maps while you're on Wi-Fi and store them on your device so you may be able to access them even without GPS or signal, but check if you can before setting out that loss of GPS or signal will not pose a problem.

It is in any case recommended that you familiarise yourself with the OS grid referencing system first, using the instructions shown on the key of every OS Explorer map.

A WALKING HOBBY FOR THE TWENTY-FIRST CENTURY – GEOCACHING

Geocaching has become a very popular pursuit, thanks to GPS. It involves seeking out and finding, using map references and GPS/navigation apps, a 'cache', usually consisting of a robust box buried in the ground, in a tree, in a summit cairn or other suitable place out of view, containing some goodies, e.g. food items/toys, and a means of logging your find. There's a strong geocaching etiquette – if you take something, you leave something behind. Some items may be passed from one cache to another, making their own journey around the country. It's a bit like a treasure hunt, combining fresh air and exercise with some detective work, and is an obsession for some; it's not unknown for geocachers to have clocked up several hundred caches. So, google 'geocaching' and join in the fun, adding another dimension to your walking enjoyment!

ABOUT FOOD AND DRINK

During the town and city walks you did, you'd have been spoilt for choice as far as refreshment opportunities went. However there aren't too many branches of Costa in the wilds of the Peak District or the Brecon Beacons.

It is essential, whether you hope or expect to pass a cafe or pub en route, that when out wild walking you have not only plenty of bottled water with you but also food supplies. On cold days, a thermos with a hot drink is advisable as well.

FOOD FOR THOUGHT

- That cafe or pub you earmarked might be unexpectedly shut.

- There may be no cafes or pubs on your route.

- You may need to replenish your energy levels at a time when you're far away from any amenities.

- Eating and drinking out is expensive – you can buy a thermos flask for little more than the price of a couple of takeaway coffees.

Ensure the food you take is rich in energy and fills you up. Hunger, like thirst, is demoralising and could disastrously diminish your stamina levels. The energy boost provided by sugary snacks such as chocolate bars or cakes will be temporary;

anything that dramatically increases your blood sugar level will result in a rebound sugar low, which gives you an energy slump. Instead, opt for healthy snacks such as nuts and fruit, especially bananas, which are rich in potassium and provide slow-releasing energy. Protein is also very good for walkers, giving you energy throughout the day.

A (slightly) naughty tip – If you can't resist sweet treats for a fix of energy, try Kendal Mint Cake. It's not cake at all, but very sweet minty confectionery and very refreshing, beloved of hill walkers. Just don't tell your dentist...

ABOUT PRECAUTIONS

Most wild walks are accomplished without difficulty or incident. But sometimes bad things happen.

The four last things that you want to happen on a wild walk:

1. Injury

2. Illness or exhaustion

3. Getting lost

4. Deterioration in weather or light

Prevention is of course, better than cure:

♦ Avoid risk of injury by being careful and sensible, being properly booted and clad, and being vigilant for obstacles and hazards.

- If you feel unwell at the start of the day, consider if it's sensible to go out.

- Avoid the risk of exhaustion by following the advice given in relation to stamina levels and taking supplies of food and drink with you for consumption when needed. Never set out to do more than you can comfortably manage in a day.

- Avoid getting lost by being proficient in map reading, using a compass and/or GPS/navigation apps.

- Don't go out, or be prepared to curtail your walk, if there is a risk of bad weather or you are short on daylight.

TOP TIPS

Top tip from the doyen of Lakeland mountain walking, Alfred Wainwright: simply, watch always where you are putting your feet. If you want to admire the view, *stop* and then admire it.

But even then, things can go wrong. So:

- Ensure you're equipped with a first-aid kit including a supply of bandages and plasters. A torch is also advisable if there is any risk of being caught out by the darkness.

- Have your mobile phone and make sure it's fully charged before you go out walking, leave your details with someone and in turn take their details, so you have a source of help if you do get stranded.

* In the event of your mobile phone failing, the recognised distress signal is six blasts of a whistle repeated at one minute intervals.

ABOUT RUCKSACKS

Even if you're just going out for a day's wild walking, there'll be a fair bit to take with you. There'll be essentials such as cash/plastic, food, drink, first-aid kit, phone and any other appropriate emergency equipment (e.g. whistle); your map, also compass or GPS device/smartphone; and you may find you have spare clothing with you that you don't need on all the time, but you need to have with you just in case.

Clearly you can't carry these things about with you in a 5p M&S bag: you will need a rucksack, big enough to accommodate what you need, but not so big that you're tempted to take a lot of stuff you don't need. The benefit of a rucksack is that it enables the weight of your load to be spread evenly and enables you to retain a good posture, ensuring that the weight on your shoulders is kept to a minimum.

Once again, you get what you pay for, but any rucksack must be capable of fitting comfortably on your back, with straps that adjust so you can reduce the weight on your shoulders, and be able to keep the contents dry.

WHERE TO GO?

So – you've equipped yourself, and you're raring to go. But where to go?

In Great Britain alone we are blessed with an amazingly wide variety of countryside, catering for the tastes of every walker. It's difficult to know where to start, but a great place to choose as the base for your wild walking in Britain is one or more of the National Parks. Here we offer a particular jewel for each crown.

THREE BITS OF NATIONAL PARK TRIVIA

- The National Parks of Britain currently receive over 150 million day visits a year

- Most recent statistics suggest that the South Downs and Lake District are the most visited

- The least visited are Northumberland and Exmoor – why not give them a visit to see what everyone's missing out on?

THE CURRENT NATIONAL PARKS OF THE UNITED KINGDOM

In England

Yorkshire Dales – James Herriot country, limestone cliffs, impressive fells interspersed with beautiful valleys such as Swaledale and Wensleydale (try the ascent of Whernside – described in full below)

Lake District – England's highest peaks and a host of other fells and mountains around the unforgettably beautiful lakes of Derwent Water, Ullswater, Wastwater and many more (try Haystacks from Buttermere, with astonishing views and the last resting place of Alfred Wainwright)

Peak District – comprises the White Peak, lush rolling green hills and picturesque dales, and the Dark Peak, forbidding yet magnificent peat moorland (try the Kinder Plateau and the Kinder Low viewpoint)

Exmoor – steep heather-clad hills and beautiful woodland, immortalised by R. D. Blackmore in the classic novel *Lorna Doone* (try Dunkery Beacon, the summit of Exmoor and Somerset)

Dartmoor – windswept, wild moorland, characterised by stony hilltops called tors (try High Willhays, the highest point in southern England – described in full below)

Northumberland – huge forests, the Cheviot hills rising to over 2,600 ft (800 m) and Hadrian's Wall (yes, try Hadrian's Wall, large sections of which have been miraculously and splendidly preserved)

North York Moors – heather moorland, sweeping views and some of the best cliff scenery on the East coast of Britain (try Roseberry Topping, the distinctive peak on the Cleveland Way)

Norfolk and Suffolk Broads – these lakes and wetlands of East Anglia are a magnet for wildlife and plant life (try a stroll round the wetland habitats of Hickling Broad National Nature Reserve near Potter Heigham)

South Downs – rolling chalk downland with sensational views to the Weald and the sea (try walking from Hassocks to Ditchling Beacon with its amazing Wealden views – described in full below)

New Forest – not only forest but fine coastal scenery with beautiful views to the Isle of Wight (try walking beside the River Beaulieu from Buckler's Hard, with its maritime museum and timeless waterside setting, to Beaulieu, with its Cistercian abbey)

In Scotland

The Cairngorms – numerous mountains over 4,000 ft (1,200 m) and two fine rivers, the Dee and the Spey (try a section of the Speyside Way, especially round Glenlivet and its association with whisky)

Loch Lomond and the Trossachs – classic Scottish Highland scenery (try the lochside walk from Balmaha to Ardlui on the West Highland Way)

In Wales

Snowdonia – the highest mountain of England and Wales, numerous lakes, magnificent coastal scenery (try Snowdon, the highest point of Wales)

Pembrokeshire Coast – some of the most stunning cliff scenery in Britain (try the walk along the Pembrokeshire Coast Path between St David's Head and St David's)

Brecon Beacons – flat-topped mountains rising to nearly 3,000 ft (900 m), contrasted with the peace and beauty of the Monmouthshire & Brecon Canal (try the ascent of Pen-y-Fan, the summit of the Beacons)

TRY THESE WILD NATIONAL PARK WALKS

Below are three wild walks for you to try, all in National Parks, very contrasting in nature and representing different parts of the country, and all hugely enjoyable. They aren't technically difficult and can each be easily accomplished in a day, but they are strenuous, they demand respect, and you need to be fit and follow the instructions given above. They're all circular walks starting from places served by public transport.

A wild walk on the South Downs to Ditchling Beacon, the highest point in East Sussex – 6 miles (9.6 km). Start – Hassocks station, West Sussex

*From **Hassocks station** walk briefly down the station approach road then opposite the pub turn right down a flight of steps to meet the main street (B2116). At the bottom, cross the road, turn right and walk towards the **railway bridge**; as you reach the bridge you meet two signed paths in close succession going off to the left. Ignore the first but take the second, which for just over a mile (1.6 km) runs parallel with and just to the left of the railway, ending by the junction of the B2112, coming in from the left, with the A273. Cross straight over the B2112 and follow a signed path over a **sports field**, aiming for the right-hand side of the clubhouse, then beyond the clubhouse join the approach road taking you very shortly to **Clayton village street**. You need to cross straight over onto a signed bridleway heading southwards, but it's worth detouring to the right to see two features of **Clayton**. One is the extraordinary brick baronial entrance to **Clayton tunnel** on the London to Brighton* line, and the other is the **village church**, which boasts a pre-1066 chancel arch and superb medieval wall paintings. Keith Spence, in his Companion Guide to Kent and Sussex, bemoans the fact that they have 'had to contend with being spattered by bat droppings!'

Now proceed along the **bridleway** south of the village street. Ignore a signed (yellow arrow) footpath going off to the left, and continue along the obvious signed (**blue arrow**) bridleway, which now gains height quickly, heading steeply southeastwards. Now look out for the two **windmills**, Jack and Jill, to your right, and aim for the clear path skirting the northeast side of the mills. Of the two, Jill, the right-hand one as you look at them, is undoubtedly the more attractive and photogenic, with its sails and bright white colour; the darker Jack, to the left, is something of a poor relation, lacking any sails! Jack is the tower of a smock mill whereas Jill is a post mill, built in 1821 and actually hauled here from Brighton in 1850 – by oxen.

Having paused to enjoy the mills, keep along the path, arriving at a T-junction where you turn left onto a clear track heading southeastwards. Very shortly the **South Downs Way** comes in from the right, and you now follow the South Downs Way all the way to **Ditchling Beacon**. Initially, you continue to climb, keeping the fence to your left, then you veer gently left, from southeastwards to just north of east, now on top of the scarp. The East Sussex/West Sussex border spur of the **Sussex Border Path** comes in, also from the right (although it isn't signed) and then shortly goes off to the left. Now enjoying magnificent views, continue along the top of the scarp, passing just to the right of clumps of bushes and one of the characteristic **dewponds** of the

*South Downs Way (SDW); you shortly pass to the left of another dewpond, then begin a very clear and quite stiff climb, signalling your approach to the climax of the walk. As you climb, you keep a fence to your right. The fence bends sharply to the right and immediately beyond this bend you'll see the **trig point** above you to the right. Now simply make your way to it. The trig point provides a tremendous panorama, stretching across the Downs for miles in both directions, the Weald to the north, and the sea to the south. In 1588 one of a chain of big fires was lit here to warn of the Spanish Armada's approach.*

*From the trig point, make your way back to the SDW and just continue a little further east to enjoy a superb view to **Blackcap**, the next big summit on the **South Downs**.*

*Now you head back towards **Hassocks** along the SDW, initially downhill then along the top of the escarpment, rising very steadily to the wooden signpost known as **Keymer Post**, roughly a mile from Ditchling Beacon. Turn right here onto the signed bridleway, which heads steeply downhill, then in roughly half a mile (800 m) veers right. At this point, fork left onto a signed path that descends through the trees to reach **Underhill Lane**, going straight over to follow a grassy path that veers to the right, keeping an attractive lake to the right. Follow the signed path through the meadow, then as the lake veers away to the right and you get within sight of the eastern end of the meadow, veer round to the left and walk up to a gate at the top end, beyond which you go forward to arrive at **Lodge Lane**. Turn left to follow it down to the B2112 **New Road**, crossing straight over and following it, arriving at the B2116 in the centre of **Keymer**, passing a particularly fine thatched and timbered* *cottage just before the junction. Keymer boasts some other fine buildings including (by detouring very briefly right) the partially timber-framed* **Greyhound Inn** *and the part-Norman church of* **St Cosmas and St Damian.** *Your route is left at the junction, past* **Keymer Manor House,** *a four-bay aisled fourteenth-century medieval house. Now follow the road to Hassocks, with its good range of shops and cafes, bearing right along the station approach road to arrive at the station.*

A wild walk on Dartmoor to High Willhays, the summit of Dartmoor and the highest ground in southern England – 9 miles (14.4 km). You can shorten the walk to 6 miles (9.6 km) by taking a car or taxi to point (1) below. Start – White Hart, Okehampton, Devon

From the **White Hart Hotel** in the centre of Okehampton, walk away from the main street up **George Street** adjacent to the hotel. The road bends slightly left; you see a church on the left, and more or less opposite the church you turn right up **Station Road**, and follow it uphill. There's a left turn signed to the old Okehampton Station but don't follow this; rather, carry straight on uphill, passing over the old railway and also the A30. There's a very sharp right-hand bend and then it's a straightforward road walk until you reach a small parking area on the right-hand side and the public road effectively ends (1). A right turn here leads to **Okehampton Camp**, while roads leading away to the left are accessible to vehicles on a permissive basis only. Bear left and then immediately right along a tarmac track, keeping **Moor Brook** immediately to your left and a wall to your right. Keeping the modest **Row Tor** to your left, remain on the tarmac track up to a junction, with the tarmac track veering sharply left and a rougher track continuing ahead. Go straight over onto this rougher track, keeping **West Mill Tor**, appreciably higher than Row Tor, to your left. Follow this rougher track onto **Black Down**, as far as a junction of paths level with a col between **West Mill Tor** and its neighbour **Yes Tor** to the right, higher still than West Mill Tor. Turn left at this junction.

You now follow what is quite a well-defined path fairly gently uphill across the moor. The gradient then gets stiffer and the *ground underfoot squelchier as you make your way up to the col between West Mill Tor and Yes Tor. When the ground levels out, look carefully for a crossroads of paths more or less level with the stones on **West Mill Tor**, which are to your left. Turn right here and now follow a path towards **Yes Tor**; it's fairly faint in places, but the path is more clearly defined up the hillside, so simply use that as a line. Initially the going is quite easy and remains so as far as **Red-a-ven Brook** which you have to ford, taking care as the stones around the brook may be quite slippery. Beyond the brook is the hardest work of the walk, as you climb very steeply to the summit of **Yes Tor** (grid reference for GPS – SX 580901), but you'll be amply rewarded. The summit is marked not only by stones but a triangulation point, and the views are astonishing, especially over **Dartmoor** but also northwards over mid-Devon towards Exmoor. It's only when you reach the summit of Yes Tor that the summit of **High Willhays** (grid reference for GPS – SX 580892) becomes apparent and the path to it, heading just west of south, is very obvious. Thankfully the col separating the two peaks is extremely shallow so the going is very easy. You descend gently and at the bottom of the descent, look out for a clear track going away to the left; don't follow it yet, but mark it, as you'll need it for the return journey! The track, meantime, climbs up, again quite gently, to arrive on the **High Willhays plateau**. There is a fair array of stones and boulders on the plateau but the proper summit is very clear, marked by a large cairn.*

Now you need to make your way off the top, and return to the junction with the clear track referred to in the paragraph above (GPS – SX 580899); in clear weather this will be very easy, but in mist it could be a great deal harder. Having reached the track at the col, turn right to follow it. It drops quite gently, keeping **Yes Tor** *to your left, and reaches the same beck that you forded earlier; again you need to ford it, and then continue on the clear stony track. Even if the mist prevented you enjoying the views on the summits, you should be luckier now, the views are quite magnificent, not only to other tors of Dartmoor and their rock-strewn tops, but the rolling green fields of mid-Devon stretching on forever. The journey may be enlivened even further by the sight of* **Dartmoor ponies.** *The track continues very obviously, keeping* **West Mill Tor** *to the left and* **Row Tor** *to the right; don't be tempted onto a track snaking to the right on the nearside of Row Tor. The track becomes tarmac, and it's now simply a matter of following it back to point (1) above and retracing your steps to* **Okehampton,** *be it by car or on foot.*

A wild walk in North Yorkshire – the ascent of Whernside, the highest point in North Yorkshire and one of the so-called Three Peaks – 7 miles (11.2 km). Start – Ribblehead Station, North Yorkshire

Walk down the station approach slip road. Turn right onto the B6255 **Hawes-Ingleton road** and pass the pub, then very shortly bear left along a signed bridleway; proceed on the wide bridleway northwestwards, parallel with the railway, then veer left under the **Ribblehead viaduct**. This magnificent construction was completed between 1870 and 1875. Go forward northwestwards along the bridleway, veering westwards to **Gunnerfleet Farm** and passing the farm buildings to reach a T-junction with a track. Turn left onto it, then very shortly bear right along a signed footpath, keeping a wall to the right; go over a ladder stile and into the next field, going half-left across this field aiming for a little gate in the wall. Proceed through the gate into the adjacent field and follow the wall, heading northwestwards uphill. Use stone slabs to cross a wall and go forward across the next field, the path indicated by the darker grass, bringing you to the buildings of **Ivescar**. Ignore a signed bridleway going hard left but go forward into the farm area itself, and arrive at a clear bridle track pointing northeast/southwest. Turn left onto it, heading southwestwards, ignoring an early fork to the right. The track is well defined initially; it reaches a gate and veers gently right, and is then rather less well defined as it veers gently left and goes forward to another gate. Beyond it, continue in pretty much the same direction to reach the buildings of **Broadrake**, which are to your right and, sticking to the same direction, continue beyond Broadrake across a field to reach a signed path junction. Turn right here along the path signed '**Whernside** 1¾ miles'.

The taxiing is now over, and you begin the assault on **Whernside** on what is a very clear path indeed, narrow but easily discernible all the way up. It is rocky and exceedingly steep in places, but the views just get better all the time. Eventually, it veers to the right, the gradient lessens, and you find yourself on the ridge. It's then a very exciting ridgetop walk to the summit triangulation point, and although the triangulation point itself is just behind a wall, you certainly won't miss it however bad the weather is. The views are magnificent; **Pen-y-ghent** and **Ingleborough** are the most distinctive and conspicuous features, but the **Ribblehead viaduct** is also clearly visible, while to the northwest the verdant **Dentdale** provides a fine contrast to the stark, steep hillsides.

Continue on beyond the summit along the ridge, sticking to the obvious main path, then within sight of the pools known as **Whernside Tarns**, you veer northeastwards and drop down steeply round the side of **Great Knoutberry Hill**. Veering southeastwards, you keep on an obvious path, which continues to descend and arrives at a T-junction of paths. Turn right to follow the path southeastwards, looking out for a lovely waterfall just to your right. Shortly you reach the railway and cross over it, but immediately to your right is a remarkable feature, a stone aqueduct carrying the stream that flows from the waterfall. Now keeping the railway to your right, and enjoying superb views to **Ingleborough** ahead, continue downhill past the **Blea Moor** signal box, arriving at a junction with the bridleway you were on at the start, close to the viaduct. You've come full *circle and it now simply remains for you to turn left onto the bridleway and walk back to Ribblehead station.*

> *'I come from haunts of coot and hern*
> *I make a sudden sally*
> *And sparkle out among the fern*
> *To bicker down a valley'*

Alfred, Lord Tennyson, *'The Brook'*

MUNRO OR MARILYN?

If you're looking for a wild walking challenge in the British Isles you could become a peak bagger, building up 'collections' of hill - or mountaintops you've managed to scale.

Munros – named after the mountaineer Hugh Munro, these are the 283 mountains in Scotland that exceed 3,000 ft (914.4 m) above sea level. Munro-bagging is very popular among keen walkers and around 5,000 people have bagged them all. Some Munros are tougher than others and some are very tough indeed, not to be attempted save by experienced, fit and properly equipped hill walkers, especially in bad weather or in winter. Incidentally, Scottish mountains of between 2,500 ft (762 m) and 3,000 ft high are known as Corbetts and those between 2,000 ft (609 m) and 2,500 ft high are Grahams!

Marilyns – a Marilyn is a hilltop with an overall drop of at least 150 m (492 ft) on all sides. Therefore even a very lofty peak (peak 1) will not be a Marilyn if there is a peak immediately adjacent (peak 2) which is higher – unless it is necessary to drop more than 150 m from the top of peak 1 to arrive at the base of peak 2. It follows, then, that in low-lying areas there will be some Marilyns of quite modest elevation, easily within the capability of even relatively inexperienced hill walkers. There are no fewer than 2,009 of them in the British Isles.

Wainwrights – these are the 214 Lake District fells described in the pictorial guides of Alfred Wainwright (whom we'll meet again in Chapter 6). You may bag only a few at a time but that gives you an excuse to keep coming back to the Lake District, which provides the most stunning mountain and lake scenery in England.

County Highs – the highest points of every county or administrative region in Great Britain. Pre-1974, British counties were straightforward to find on a map but the establishment of unitary authorities has massively complicated things. However, complete lists are available in book form and on the internet, and bagging them all provides a worthy objective for the hill walker, as well as walks of remarkable variety – from the modest ascent of Beacon Hill in Norfolk to the grandeur of Mickle Fell in County Durham or Scafell Pike in Cumbria. In between there are such gems as Worcestershire Beacon in the Malvern Hills, Cleeve Hill in the Cotswolds and even Hampstead Heath, the highest point in inner London, with stunning views across the capital.

Did you know that in 2006 Jonny Muir in three months visited the 91 historic county tops of the British Isles in a 5,000-mile (8,000-km) walk? And in 2010 Alan Hinkes – the first Briton to climb the 14 highest peaks on the planet – scaled the highest points of the 39 traditional counties of England in eight days in a continuous walk starting at The Cheviot and ending on Helvellyn.

Just because it's not in a National Park or isn't a peak doesn't mean it's not worth exploring. Armed with your map, your equipment and the advice above, you can build up your own portfolio of wild walks and learn to love the immense variety of the scenery of Great Britain, and, with appropriate mapping and guidebooks, do the same overseas – through the joy of walking.

Did you know that there was only one hill Alfred Wainwright decided was *not* worth climbing? Black Hill, West Yorkshire, on the Pennine Way.

WILDER WALKING OVERSEAS

The National Park concept isn't just confined to Great Britain: there are National Parks, as defined by the International Union for the Conservation of Nature (a joint government/non-government body which provides knowledge and tools for human progress, economic development and nature conservation to take place in harmony), all over the world.

Though marine parks and safari parks are plainly unsuitable for walkers, there are still hundreds of wonderful National Parks for walkers to enjoy. Here's our top four, followed by our pick of the rest in no particular order:

Yellowstone National Park is the daddy of them all. This was the first National Park in the USA, being inaugurated as a National Park in 1872. A wilderness recreation area which extends for 3,500 square miles (9,000 square km), it's situated on the top of a volcanic hot spot and comprises a massive variety of natural phenomena, including dramatic canyons, alpine rivers, gushing geysers (including Old Faithful) and hot springs. Among the wildlife to be found here are bears, wolves, bison, elk and antelopes. There are 900 miles (1,450 km) of walking trails around the park for you to enjoy.

Torres del Paine National Park is located in central Patagonia, Chile, inaugurated as a National Park in 1959 and covering 700 square miles (1,814 square km). Of the park's many stunning geographical features, the most spectacular are arguably the towering jagged mountain peaks. Complementing the mountain scenery are blue icebergs, glaciers and grasslands known as pampas, which shelter rare wildlife such as guanacos, creatures that resemble llamas.

Yosemite National Park is situated just a few hours east of San Francisco, USA, in California's Sierra Nevada mountains. It was inaugurated as a National Park in 1890 and covers 1,169 square miles (3,027 square km). It is famed for its giant sequoia trees, the tallest trees in the world, and for Tunnel View, the astonishing vista of the huge Bridalveil Fall and the granite cliffs of Half Dome and El Capitan.

Grand Canyon National Park in Arizona, USA, inaugurated as a National Park in 1919, is home to arguably the most spectacular chasm in the world, with its incredibly deep drops and unique rock formations, consisting of layered tiers of red chalk – a geological history lesson stretching back millions of years. The National Park covers 1,904 square miles (4,950 square km), its viewpoints including Lipan Point and Mather Point.

And so to the remainder, all of them providing great walking opportunities for the more adventurous hiker. However, much of the terrain covered by National Parks is inhospitable and potentially hazardous, so even if there are no restrictions on independent travel you may wish to explore the possibility of guided walks.

- ARENAL VOLCANO NATIONAL PARK, Costa Rica, with an active volcano surrounded by stunning landscapes

- IGUAZU NATIONAL PARK, Argentina and Brazil, an area of rainforest with amazing waterfalls

- BANFF NATIONAL PARK, Canada, with its lakes, glaciers and peaks

- KRKA NATIONAL PARK, Croatia, famed for its forests and waterfalls

- TULUM NATIONAL PARK, Mexico, with its ancient Mayan ruins and beaches with nesting turtles

- JIUZHAIGOU VALLEY NATIONAL PARK, China, with its lakes, evergreen forests and dazzling autumn colours

- GOREME NATIONAL PARK, Turkey, famous for its rock homes and so-called fairy chimneys

- PANTANAL MATOGROSSENSE NATIONAL PARK, Brazil, one of the world's largest tropical wetlands with wildlife including the caiman and capybara

- CINQUE TERRE NATIONAL PARK, Italy with its forests, hiking trails and villages on the Italian Riviera

- SNOWDONIA NATIONAL PARK, North Wales, the only National Park in Great Britain to make the list; it includes Snowdon (Wales's highest mountain), and has the dazzling village of Portmeirion right on its doorstep

- JASPER NATIONAL PARK, Canada, with its mixture of forests, glaciers and wildlife

- FIORDLAND NATIONAL PARK, New Zealand with its fjords and waterfalls

- NAMIB-NAUKLUFT NATIONAL PARK, Namibia, where hiking trails lead you to sand dunes the size of skyscrapers

- PLITVICE LAKES NATIONAL PARK, Croatia, with its chain of 16 terraced lakes joined by waterfalls

- KOMODO NATIONAL PARK, Indonesia, where you'll find the world's largest lizard, the Komodo dragon

- GUILIN-LIJIANG RIVER NATIONAL PARK, Southeast China, with its remarkable rock formations known as karsts

- CANAIMA NATIONAL PARK, Venezuela, which includes the iconic Angel Falls (NOTE: at the time of writing the political situation in Venezuela is extremely unstable and you should take advice from the Foreign Office as to whether it is safe to travel there)

- EVERGLADES NATIONAL PARK, Florida, USA, where alligators dwell among the wetlands

- JOSTEDALSBREEN NATIONAL PARK, Norway, which includes the astonishing Briksdalsbreen Glacier

- KILIMANJARO NATIONAL PARK, Tanzania, with Africa's highest mountain

- TAYRONA NATIONAL PARK, Colombia, with its virgin jungle, monkeys and coral reefs

- LOS GLACIARES NATIONAL PARK, Argentina, home to the Perito Moreno Glacier

- GALAPAGOS NATIONAL PARK, Ecuador, where tortoises and iguanas dwell among the coral reefs, and where you'll find cacti forests and lava trails

THERE OUGHT TO BE A WORD FOR IT (2)

Keen walker's Christmas slide show, a cherished but paradoxically dreaded tradition amongst his nearest and dearest, consisting of many years' worth of inferior images projected using outdated or wholly unreliable technology

Post-Christmas-lunch walk organised by a keen walker for his family and house guests, inevitably far longer than any of them have walked in a single stretch this year

Involuntary reliving by insomniac of his long and tiring previous day's walk, so that by the time morning comes he's re-walked it 28 times

Disappointment mingled with huge anticlimax that you feel on successfully reaching end of very long and challenging walk and finding everyone in your destination town or village going about their business without any recognition of you or what you've achieved

Chagrin on finding you're half a stone heavier after long walk than you were before it, on account of mixed grill, death by chocolate and two bottles of wine with which you celebrated its completion

State of total denial into which you move on reaching fog-enveloped hilltop after a 4-hour climb, in which you refuse to believe that the fog is not only still there but if anything is even thicker than when you started

Unavoidable sense of smugness you feel when enjoying walking holiday in utterly remote, unspoilt countryside and seeing newspaper picture of heatwave crowds packed on Brighton beach with no more than one square metre of space per person

Urge, having reached a particularly great viewpoint or other famous landmark on your walk, to use your mobile to smugly ring a work colleague who you know is hard at work and tell them what a great time you're having

Sense of infuriation when scheduled televised Wainwright walk is postponed owing to overrunning of friendly international football match

Expression of disappointment that the first person to sign your marathon walk sponsor form pledges 50p on completion of the whole expedition

5 | LONG-DISTANCE WALKING

'I staggered on as if in a dream… Why had my boots become lead weights and my legs turned to jelly?'

Alan Plowright, *Plowright Follows Wainwright*

'There must be something about long-distance walking that compels some people to keep trekking when they'd be better advised to quit.'

Paddy Dillon, *The National Trails*

So far we've only really considered day-length walks. Now we turn to the many opportunities available both in Britain and abroad for you to put together several days' walking and accomplish one of the many long-distance routes that have been devised and mapped by walkers past and present.

Before looking at the long-distance routes available, we need to consider the practicalities of walking on several consecutive days. Undertaking and completing the challenge of a long-distance walk is a very satisfying experience for a walker but it is not a challenge to be undertaken lightly.

To successfully complete a long-distance walk requires you to combine all the walking skills detailed in Chapters 3 and 4 together with three others:

1.   A high level of physical fitness

2.   Excellent organisation

3.   The right equipment

A HIGH LEVEL OF PHYSICAL FITNESS

We've already looked at the importance of building up your stamina levels but there's a difference between a single day's or afternoon's strenuous walk which you can recover from over time, and having to get walking again the next morning. You don't need to be super-fit to complete a long-distance route, but it stands to reason that if your route of choice is 180 miles (288 km) and you can only manage 5 miles (8 km) a day, it's going to take you an awfully long time to complete it. Unless you're happy to take that long over a single path, you need to improve your daily quota, doing this by regular, frequent walking, ensuring your footwear is not only appropriate but comfortable, endeavouring as far as possible to replicate the terrain you're likely to meet on your route of choice (including carrying the equivalent weight and volume of equipment you'll need), and following the advice on sensible eating – to ensure not only that your body is up to it but you eat sensibly while out on the walks themselves. Your training regime should include a number of consecutive days' walking so you get used to the discipline of walking day after day after day.

EXCELLENT ORGANISATION

Planning a long-distance walk is hugely enjoyable but it must be done sensibly.

Having decided what route you are thinking of tackling, go to the Long Distance Walkers Association website, which offers information on pretty much every named long-distance footpath in Great Britain. Alternatively, visit your local library or bookshop to see what literature there is in relation to your path of choice. Whether you go online or use a guidebook, build up a picture of the total route length, the likely detours you'll want or need to make, and, crucially, the nature of the terrain you will encounter.

+ Now you need to consider carefully:

+ How many consecutive days' walking are available to you?

and

+ How many miles do you think you can manage on each of them?

You'll have a good idea from your training regime how many miles you can comfortably walk in a day, given the terrain you're up against. It's very important to be realistic and err on the side of underestimating rather than overestimating your daily mileage. You may end up overdoing it and having to give up halfway through. Better to aim to do a manageable amount in the time available then look forward to returning to it in a few months. Remember – it's not going to go away!

Of course there's nothing to stop you doing the whole of a long-distance route in separate day excursions, but you may feel the continuity will suffer, and if you live a long way from the route you may end up spending more in petrol and fares than on accommodation.

If you decide to do several consecutive days' walking on a long-distance route, there will inevitably be some days that require you to do more mileage than others because of the availability of accommodation or public transport at particular points.

There are some long-distance routes where 'staging posts' are very many miles apart with no public transport, amenities or accommodation in between, and where you would have to walk many miles to obtain them. Such as:

- On Glyndwr's Way – 28 miles (45 km) between Llanidloes and Machynlleth

- On the Southern Upland Way – 27 miles (43 km) between St John's Town of Dalry and Sanquhar

- On the Pennine Way – 27 miles (43 km) between Byrness and Kirk Yetholm

Accommodation is of course a matter of personal taste. Camping costs next to nothing and allows you to be wholly independent, but after a long day's walking you may not relish the idea of pitching a tent, particularly in bad weather. At the other extreme, a luxury hotel provides the perfect chance to unwind but will do your budget no favours. Many walkers opt for something in between, either youth hostelling or a B & B/guest house. Youth hostels used to have a reputation for being formidably Spartan establishments with dour wardens, compulsory morning duties, lack of creature comforts and strict rules. That is no longer the case: generally nowadays they are very comfortable, have more than adequate facilities and are excellent value for money. Many lasting walking friendships have sprung from youth hostel life. (For avoidance of doubt, don't be put off by the word 'youth' as anyone's eligible to stay in 'youth' hostels!) A B & B, a very British institution, will offer friendly hospitality, a comfortable room and a delicious breakfast to set you up for your day's walk. Note that the term 'guest house' is confusing: some establishments calling themselves guest houses offer exactly the same hospitality as B & Bs, but with other establishments there may be no breakfast available, merely kitchen facilities, and the owner may not actually live on the premises. It's advisable to book ahead to avoid spending time at the end of a long day's walk looking for a place to stay; it's pretty much the norm now for any establishment, regardless of the type of accommodation, to accept online booking.

DISTANCE LEARNING – FOUR TOP TIPS

* **Top tip 1**: when booking your B & B, check how far it is from the route of your path – you don't want to add a lot of dead mileage to your daily quota!

- **Top tip 2**: Make sure you have with you the addresses and phone numbers of your accommodations, and if you're relying on lifts or public transport, relevant contact numbers and times. It's a good idea to text your accommodation provider to let them know you are on your way and confirm arrival time; this may save a lot of waiting around outside your accommodation when you would rather be enjoying a hot bath or shower inside!

- **Top tip 3**: Always think and plan ahead; think about when you might need supplies and where you're going to get them. If it's clear from your map or guide that there's going to be nowhere to buy food or drink during your day's walk, stock up beforehand.

- **Top tip 4**: Investigate whether, if you're undertaking one of the more popular long-distance walks, a bag-carrying service is available – you will certainly make faster progress if you're not having to carry all your equipment.

THE RIGHT EQUIPMENT

In Chapter 4 we considered what you'll need to take with you on a day's wild walking, and all that – and more – applies when you're walking for several days at a time and are away from home. You'll need a much bigger rucksack, with a belt round your middle so you're not carrying the weight on your shoulders. Then you'll need your checklist to help you load it up.

YOUR LONG-DISTANCE WALK EQUIPMENT CHECKLIST

- Navigational aids, paper or electronic
- Cash/plastic
- Phone with charger (and camera if your phone can't take pictures!)
- Contact/accommodation details (whether stored in your phone or on paper)
- Food supplies
- First-aid kit plus other emergency kit, e.g. whistle, torch
- Changes of clothing/footwear
- Toiletries
- Binoculars
- Sunglasses
- Sunblock/sun hat
- Colder weather: gloves/scarf/woolly hat
- Diary/journal to record your experiences – and pen/pencil
- And – if you've decided to camp – all your camping equipment

A word to the wise: If having loaded all these into your rucksack you can't lift it up off the floor, don't panic. Take out everything you feel you can manage without. If after that you still can't lift it up off the floor – then you can panic...

HOW TO LIGHTEN THAT RUCKSACK LOAD

- Make quite sure there's nothing in there left over from a previous expedition.

- Make use of all the pockets and compartments on your rucksack – you may not even realise they're there.

- Pack lighter clothes for evening wear.

- See if it's practicable for any equipment/clothes etc to be sent on to you during the walk – with you sending 'used' equipment home at the same time.

- Consider whether you can do without any reading books – many hotels and B & Bs are well stocked with reading material, and there's always Kindle!

- Consider what might fit into the pockets of your jacket or even round your neck, e.g. binoculars, map case.

Sod's Law dictates: It's always the one item you need the most that will inevitably find its way into the most inaccessible part of your rucksack.

CHOOSING YOUR LONG-DISTANCE WALK

The Ordnance Survey Explorer maps reveal a vast number of long-distance routes in Great Britain alone. The choice is bewildering, and they vary tremendously in length, difficulty, quality of signposting and amount of literature available.

Long-distance routes in Great Britain can be subdivided as follows:

- National Trails (England and Wales)

- Scotland's Great Trails

- Other 'named' paths, well established and maintained, sometimes referred to on maps and on book covers as recreational paths

- Less well-established and maintained named paths

- And we also need to mention the small matter of LEJOG or JOGLE!

Did you know that in the 1996 film *Trainspotting,* three of the characters go on a 'healthy hike' to Rannoch Moor, which is part of the West Highland Way?

NATIONAL TRAILS (ENGLAND AND WALES)

These are state funded and generally very well maintained and signed, using the distinctive acorn logo. Every trail has a path manager who keeps in contact with the authorities that have funding and manpower available to deal with issues relating to that trail. Some of the trails have 'path associations', which issue publications and information and offer certificates or badges for successful completion. The course of every National Trail is clearly shown on the OS Explorer map. Though signage is generally good, navigational skills will still be required; no National Trail can realistically be walked on signage alowne.

These are the National Trails, from shortest to longest: (ATTC – avcragc time to complete)

Yorkshire Wolds Way (79 miles/126 km, Hessle to Filey) – an undulating walk through unspoilt chalk uplands, characterised by steep dry valleys and lush pasture. Moderately difficult. ATTC 6 days

Hadrian's Wall Path (84 miles/134 km, Wallsend to Bowness-on-Solway) – a walk beside one of the most ancient man-made features in Britain through often stunning countryside. Strenuous in places. ATTC 7 days

Ridgeway (86 miles/138 km, Overton Hill to Ivinghoe Beacon) – a journey along ancient downland tracks through Wiltshire and Berkshire then a wider variety of landscapes in the Chiltern Hills. Easy. ATTC 6 days

Peddars Way and Norfolk Coast Path (95 miles/153 km, Knettishall Heath to Cromer) – a stretch of old Roman road through Breckland and level Norfolk countryside then gentle coastal scenery. Easy. ATTC 7 days

South Downs Way (96–99 miles/155–160 km, Winchester to Eastbourne) – a well-defined route along the chalk ridges of the South Downs, with spectacular views to the Weald and the sea. Moderately difficult. ATTC 8 days

Cotswold Way (102 miles/163 km, Bath to Chipping Campden) – an up-and-down journey along the Cotswold escarpment, glorious views, beautiful villages and small towns. Moderately difficult. ATTC 8 days

Cleveland Way (108 miles/172 km, Helmsley to Filey) – a traverse of the fringes of the North York Moors followed by a walk along some of the most spectacular coastal scenery in Eastern England. Strenuous. ATTC 8 days

North Downs Way (125–130 miles/200–208 km, Farnham to Dover) – a walk along the escarpment of the North Downs through Surrey and Kent with fine views to the Weald and north towards London. Moderately difficult. ATTC 11 days

Pennine Bridleway (205 miles/330 km, Middleton Top to Ravenstonedale near Kirkby Stephen) – a traverse of the Pennines on gentler paths, suitable for riders, cyclists and walkers. Moderately difficult. ATTC 15 days

Glyndwr's Way (134 miles/214 km, Knighton to Welshpool) – an often rugged tramp through the heart of the remote mid-Wales countryside in the steps of Owain Glyndwr. Strenuous. ATTC 9 days.

Pembrokeshire Coast Path (177 miles/283 km, St Dogmaels to Amroth) – a walk along the often uneven but spectacular coastline of Southwest Wales, now a National Park. Strenuous. ATTC 14 days. NOTE: The whole route has been subsumed into the Wales Coast Path (see below)

Offa's Dyke Path (178 miles/284 km, Sedbury to Prestatyn) – a superbly varied coast-to-coast walk following the England–Wales border based on the eighth-century Offa's Dyke earthwork. Strenuous in places. ATTC 12 days

Thames Path (185 miles/296 km, Source to Thames Barrier) – following the River Thames for almost all of its length, from tranquil, unspoilt watermeadows to the bustling heart of London. Easy. ATTC 13 days

Pennine Way (260 miles/320 km, Edale to Kirk Yetholm) – the father of all the National Trails, the first to open; a very demanding walk through the Dark Peak, Yorkshire Dales and up into the Cheviots. Severe. ATTC 19 days

South West Coast Path (630 miles/1,008 km, Minehead to Poole) – our longest National Trail, following the stunning coastal/cliff scenery of Somerset, Devon, Cornwall and Dorset. Strenuous, severe in places. ATTC 7 weeks

The next National Trail scheduled to open (in 2020) will be the England Coast Path, a walk round the entire English coastline. It is expected to be 2,800 miles (4,500 km) in length. Some sections have already opened.

SCOTLAND'S GREAT TRAILS

Originally there were four Scottish official long-distance routes, branded as such, maintained and funded in similar ways to National Trails, using the thistle as a waymark. These were the original Scottish official long-distance routes:

Great Glen Way (73 miles/117 km, Fort William to Inverness) – a superbly waymarked walk along the Great Glen in the Scottish Highlands, mostly beside lochs and the Caledonian Canal. Easy. ATTC 6 days

Speyside Way (80 miles/128 km, Buckie to Aviemore) – a delightful walk through the whisky centre of Great Britain. Easy. ATTC 6 days

West Highland Way (93 miles/149 km, Milngavie to Fort William) – a walk through fine Scottish Highland scenery using well-established paths and tracks. Strenuous in places. ATTC 7 days

Southern Upland Way (212 miles/340 km, Portpatrick to Cockburnspath) – a coast-to-coast walk across high level and often very remote terrain of southern Scotland. Strenuous. ATTC 13 days

These four have now been joined by (at the time of writing) 22 other long-distance routes in Scotland to make up a total of 26 Great Trails in Scotland. The qualifications for a Great Trail are that it must be at least 25 miles (40 km) long and be 'well signed and managed', but there is no standardised signage or branding such as the acorn (as used for National Trails in England and Wales) or thistle (used on the 'original four' Scottish long-distance routes). Among the longer Great Trails are the Rob

Roy Way, the Kintyre Way and the Fife Coastal Path. Routes of the Great Trails are shown on OS Explorer maps. Again, though signage of the Trails is often extremely good, they can't be realistically walked on signage alone, and navigational skills will be required.

OTHER NAMED PATHS,
WELL ESTABLISHED AND MAINTAINED

There are a huge number of such paths in Great Britain. They appear on Explorer maps and in guidebooks, and can be found on the internet. Cicerone publish a complete directory (see Appendix). It is possible that some could be 'promoted' to National Trail or Scotland's Great Trails status in the future. Among the longest and/or best known in England and Wales are:

The Dales Way – a 95-mile (152-km) walk from Leeds to Windermere, again passing through the Yorkshire Dales, over the Pennines and into the Lake District

The London Loop – a 150-mile (241-km) walk, a sort of M25 for walkers but with fewer traffic cones and much prettier countryside, encircling the capital; and its younger brother the Capital Ring, a 78-mile (125-km) circular walk around inner London

Coast to Coast – a 192-mile (307-km) walk devised by Alfred Wainwright from St Bees on the west coast of England to Robin Hood's Bay on the east coast. It is more popular than many National Trails, passing as it does through the Lake District, Yorkshire Dales and North York Moors.

The Monarch's Way – a 615-mile (984-km) stroll from Powick Bridge in Worcestershire to Shoreham-by-Sea in West Sussex based on the route taken by King Charles II when fleeing Parliamentary forces

… and, most recently of all, The Wales Coast Path – an 870-mile (1,392-km) walk round the entire coastline of Wales, from Chepstow in the south to Queensferry in the north, incorporating stunning coastal scenery which includes the whole of the Pembrokeshire Coast Path National Trail

Which leaves us with…

LESS WELL-ESTABLISHED AND MAINTAINED NAMED PATHS

There are huge numbers of these all over Great Britain, too numerous to properly document, many established by local walking groups. In theory it's possible for any individual or walking group, with co-operation from the authorities responsible for maintaining path signage, to establish their own named path, using existing rights of way, and publicise it. With the help of social media you could even create and publicise your own long-distance walk!

Ideas for your own long-distance walk might include:

- A walk round the boundary of your county

- A walk linking every castle of your county

- A walk linking two or more cathedrals

- A walk linking two or more villages or towns of the same name

- A walk beside the longest-flowing river in your county (however far it goes – but remember, the Thames has already been done!)

- A walk linking monastic sites of the same foundation (Tony Hewitt of Cheadle, Cheshire, has devised an 'Augustinian Way' linking 35 monastic sites of Augustinian foundation, 1,140 miles/1,824 km in length from Pegwell Bay in Kent to Silloth Bay in Cumbria)

◆ A walk linking two extremes in Britain – the longest coast-to-coast, the longest line of latitude walk, etc (Tony Hewitt has also devised walks around these themes)

LEJOG OR JOGLE

The walk from Land's End to John o'Groats (LEJOG) or the other way round (JOGLE) – or simply 'end-to-end' – is not an official long-distance walk. Although it was first undertaken in the nineteenth century, it was in 1960 that this walk first really caught the public imagination when Billy Butlin – better known for his holiday camp – organised a challenge walk from 'end-to-end' with 138 finishers out of 715 starters. Since then, despite the lack of a waymarked route, it's an ambition for many walkers and a great means of raising money for charity.

How to do LEJOG

◆ By road – it's reckoned that the shortest distance by road is around 814 miles (1,302 km) *but* this does include sections of motorway, where walking is prohibited

◆ Conversely, seeking to avoid *all* roads as John Hillaby did (see Chapter 6 below)

◆ Using National Trails or other long-distance routes (a popular 'menu' is sections of South West Coast Path, Offa's Dyke Path, Pennine Way, West Highland Way and Great Glen Way) and the most direct convenient public footpath links between these sections

+ Following the coastline all the way as John Merrill did (see Chapter 6)

All the advice in relation to long-distance walking applies to an end-to-end walk but two additional aspects need to be considered. To the mileage 'on the ground' needs to be added the numerous additional miles required to access accommodation and sustenance – you can't possibly carry all the food you'll need en route. Also consider whether you start at Land's End – with the advantage of the prevailing wind on your back – or at John o'Groats – with the psychological plus of it appearing to be downhill all the way.

Did you know that the youngest person ever to walk from Land's End to John o'Groats is Joe Lambert, at the age of nine, back in 1993. It took him 40 days.

TOP TIP

If you've a serious interest in long-distance walking in Britain why not join the LDWA (Long Distance Walkers Association)? It is intended for 'people with the common interest of walking long distances in rural, mountain or moorland areas'. By joining the LDWA and attaching to one of the 43 groups in Britain that are affiliated to it, you'll be able to meet like-minded people and obtain/exchange advice and form further walking friendships.

LONG-DISTANCE WALKING OVERSEAS

'To see a world in a grain of sand,
And a heaven in a wild flower;
Hold infinity in the palm of your hand
And eternity in an hour.'

William Blake, 'Auguries of Innocence'

While in Great Britain we are blessed with an astonishing variety of landscapes, we don't have the extremes that other countries do, and which offer even richer and more challenging opportunities for the long-distance walker.

If you thought the above walks were challenging, here's our list of contenders for the top long-distance walking experiences around the world. Once you've become accustomed to wild *and* long-distance walking in Great Britain, why not try one – or more?

Inca Trail – regarded as the number 1 hiking trail in the world, there's actually a choice of trails, the most popular of which is the 'classic', going from Cuzco and leading to Machu Picchu, with mountains, rivers, lakes on your way as well as relics of the Incan civilisation. This trail is so popular that only 500 people are allowed on it per day. Distances vary depending on which of the Inca trails you opt for, but, for example, a four-day walk covers roughly 28 miles (45 km), which tells you how tough the terrain is.

The Laugavegur – this famous 34-mile (55-km) trekking route in southwest Iceland typically takes up to four days, featuring hot springs, a glacial valley, and spectacular mountains and river crossings.

Monte Fitz Roy – located in Los Glaciares National Park in the Patagonia region of South America, this is a trail of around 40 miles (64 km) past lakes, mountains and glaciers.

West Coast Trail – this 75-mile (120-km) trail in the Pacific Rim National Park runs from Bamfield to Port Renfrew in Canada. There's a great diversity of scenery, including waterfalls, forests and beaches, and wild animals including bears, wolves, sealions and cougars.

Annapurna Circuit – varying between 100 and 145 miles (160 and 230 km), this trail in Nepal and the Himalayas travels through subtropical valleys, the deepest gorge in the world, Buddhist villages and Hindu holy sites.

Franconia Ridge Loop/Traverse – this trail, in New Hampshire, USA, is just 9 miles (14 km) long but the combination of jaw-dropping panoramas, life-in-your-hands ridge traverses culminating in the 5,260-ft (1,603-m) Mount Lafayette, and miniature wild flowers, is an astonishing experience and has been called a rite of passage for explorers.

John Muir Trail – a 215-mile (346-km) journey, named after a naturalist and advocate of wilderness preservation in the USA, this western USA trail runs from Yosemite National Park to Mount Whitney, the highest peak in the continental US, via forests, glaciers, mountains and lakes.

Dosewallips to Lake Quinault in Olympic National Park, Washington, USA – this trail of 34 miles (54 km) comprises beautiful temperate rainforest, alpine meadows and snowfields, and the possibility of seeing black bears and elk.

The so-called Triple Crown of US trails consisting of:

The Continental Divide Trail – this trail of 3,100 miles (5,000 km) links Mexico and Canada and follows the Continental Divide along the Rockies, traversing Montana, Idaho, Wyoming, Colorado and New Mexico.

The Appalachian Trail – this trail of 2,178 miles (3,505 km) runs from Georgia to Maine on the eastern side of the USA. Throughout the journey you'll take approximately five million steps, cross through 14 of the eastern states and see eight National Forests and six National Parks.

The Pacific Crest Trail – passing through the western states of Washington, Oregon and California some 150 miles (240 km) east of the Pacific coast, this trail is 2,650 miles (4,240 km) long, beginning in the E. C. Manning Provincial Park in British Columbia and ending in the hot, dry Mojave area of California. It passes through an astonishing seven different National Parks. Highlights, and there are many, include the 13,153-ft (4,010-m) Forester Pass, Yosemite National Park and the great mountain ranges of Sierra Nevada and Cascade with its volcanoes.

And you thought the South West Coast Path was long!

SEVEN UNIQUE WALKING TRAILS AROUND THE WORLD

Unique for its views of the top of the world – Everest Base Camp trek (Nepal)

This is a 40-mile (64-km) trail, starting from Lukla and finishing at Everest Base Camp. The undoubted USP for this trail is the opportunity to view Mount Everest, the summit of Planet Earth. The trail passes through the heart of the Khumbu region, and you will travel in the shadow of jagged, snow-capped Himalayan peaks that would dwarf the highest mountains of any other country. It's not just the sight of these peaks that will please the eye but also the magnificent vegetation, which includes orchids and rhododendrons that are at their best in May, one of the most popular months for walking in the Himalayas. The trail passes through the village of Namche Bazaar and goes by the Buddhist monastery of Pangboche, both offering opportunities to sample and experience the Khumbu culture, and culminates in arrival at Base Camp, at 17,650 ft (5,381 m) – Everest is a mere 11,000 ft (3,353 m) higher than that! A separate day hike to Kala Pattar offers a great view not only of the summit of Everest but the Khumbu ice fall. Rather than simply returning the way you came, you could loop up and over the Cho La Pass to reveal the amazing Gokyo valley. The trek can be and has been done independently and no guided tour is necessary, but clearly you have to have appropriate levels of fitness and equipment – google 'Everest base camp trek independent' for more advice.

Unique for circling the summit of Western Europe – Tour du Mont Blanc (France, Italy, Switzerland)

The circling of Mont Blanc, at 15,781 ft (4,811 m) the highest mountain not only in the Alps but in the whole of Western Europe, is described by Topher Gaylord for National Geographic as 'one of the most special hiking experiences in the world'. The trail travels through three countries, France, Italy and Switzerland, and over several mountain passes as well as viewing some of the most dramatic glaciers. This is a 100-mile (160-km) trail, approximately, which some have done in three or four days; you may take three times that, as you walk in the shadow of impressive peaks and glaciers, stroll through blossom-filled meadows (making spring an ideal season for this walk), plunge down into seven different valleys, and of course climb back up the other side, climb to the 8,478-ft (2,584-m) summit of Fenêtre d'Arpette in Switzerland, or, to quote Topher Gaylord again, '(teeter) on spine-tingling sections of exposed rock'. And of course you may want to stop off to enjoy the many local delicacies, including fondue, home-made bread, cheese and wine. Bon appetit!

Unique for its navigational challenges – Long Range Traverse (Canada)

It may seem contradictory to describe a trail as being unique for it not being a trail at all, but this is the case with the Long Range Traverse in Newfoundland, Canada. It is only 25 miles (40 km) long, which sounds like a weekend project and no more, but the length gives no clue as to its toughness. The walk is in the Long Range Mountains near the Gulf of St Lawrence along Newfoundland's Great Northern Peninsula, starting from the fjord of Western Brook Pond and continuing to the 2,644-ft (806-m) granite dome of Gros Morne Mountain, one of the highest in the Newfoundland and Labrador province of Canada. And here's the real catch – the trail is unmarked, traversing the expanse of mountains in the Gros Morne National Park, where it is imperative that the walker is skilled in use of map and compass: it's a wilderness landscape, populated mostly by moose and caribou. But the rewards – from the blue waters that sparkle from the coastal fjords, to the spectacular if uncompromising granite cliffs, from hidden lakes to spruce groves – are infinite.

Unique for its Australasian wildlife experience – Overland Track (Tasmania)

The Overland Track in Tasmania is just 40 miles (64 km) long (although it's possible to vary the route so it increases to 50 miles (80 km)) and passes through some of the wildest and most beautiful terrain in the world, totally unspoilt and offering a solitude and remoteness that is astonishing. The trail traverses the Tasmanian World Heritage Area and boasts a phenomenal array of landscapes, including lakes, mountains, rainforests and eucalyptus groves. It includes the World Heritage-listed Cradle Mountain-Lake St Clair National Park, and it's possible to incorporate the 5,305-ft (1,617-m) Mount Ossa into your itinerary, as well as a hike round Lake St Clair. However, the real USP for this trail is the Australasian wildlife, which includes wombat, platypus and the Tasmanian devil, the largest carnivorous marsupial on the planet.

Unique for walking a country from top to bottom – Te Araroa trail (New Zealand)
Te Araroa is Maori for 'The Long Pathway' and this trail is certainly that. It is a whopping 1,864 miles (2,982 km) long and is likely to take five months to complete. But the reward for completing it is the knowledge that you have crossed the whole of New Zealand from top to bottom. The trail literally cuts through the middle of it, starting from Cape Reinga at the top of North Island, and ending at Bluff at the bottom of South Island. Don't worry – you won't be expected to walk on water between the two islands – but you will be following a total of 160 tracks into which the trail is split. Highlights of this mammoth undertaking include the river valleys soaked in Maori culture in North Island's Whanganui National Park, walking over the slopes of the active Tongariro volcano, and meandering through the Takitimu Forest, described by Dan Ransom for National Geographic as 'other-worldly'.

Unique for following the trails of animals – Caribou Tracks (USA)
This walk could range from 120 to 400 miles (192 to 640 km) – you cannot be certain. The reason is that you are, for this

journey, following literally in the steps of migrating caribou in the Gates of the Arctic National Park and the Arctic National Wildlife Refuge, both in Alaska, the most northwesterly and arguably the wildest US state of all. You are invited to witness what's been described as a wildlife miracle as massive herds of caribou move together across these areas. Not surprisingly, the walks are under the supervision of guides!

Unique as being the longest of all: the Great Trail (Canada)
This is a mind-boggling 14,193 miles (22,709 km) long, formerly known as the Trans Canada Trail. Officially completed in August 2017, it meanders around southeast Canada before performing a huge loop up to Yukon and back before finishing near Vancouver, linking up Canada's Arctic and Pacific coasts. Roughly a quarter of the trail utilises walkways or navigates wetlands on which walkers must swap boots for boats. The trail was conceived in 1992 and has taken nearly 500 volunteer groups to inaugurate.

PILGRIMAGE WALKING

One very popular form of trail walking with a purpose is pilgrimage walking. As walking has increased in popularity, so there has been an increase in walkers tracing ancient pilgrimage routes. Such journeys put walkers in touch with our spiritual past, and provide a real sense of purpose and achievement. Ancient pilgrimage routes can vary tremendously in origin, length and terrain, and the nine listed below provide a cross-section of some of the very best. Whatever your own spiritual leaning, why not try one for yourself?

The Pilgrim's Way – This is the classic pilgrimage route in England, stretching for 119 miles (192 km). It links Winchester in Hampshire with Canterbury in Kent, associated with two of the most important saints who brought Christianity to England, St Swithun (Winchester) and St Augustine (Canterbury). In ancient times, pilgrims would travel to Canterbury along prehistoric trackways to view the shrine of Thomas à Becket, infamously murdered in Canterbury Cathedral. Nowadays, thanks to modern housing developments and motorways, the original route is hard for walkers to follow, although there is signage in places, and many walkers prefer to follow the North Downs Way National Trail, which follows close to and very roughly parallel with the Pilgrim's Way from Farnham to Canterbury albeit tending to use higher ground.

The North Wales Pilgrim's Way – This runs for 130 miles (208 km) from Holy Well, called the 'Lourdes of Wales', to Bardsey Island off the Lleyn Peninsula in far northwest Wales, known as the 'island of 20,000 saints'. This has been a pilgrimage route ever since the Middle Ages but it is only since 2014 that it has been a proper waymarked route incorporating sections of the Wales Coast Path (see p.134) as well as passing through Snowdonia. The last part of the walk consists of a superb trek along the north coast of the Lleyn Peninsula.

Via Francigena – In a sense this carries on where the Pilgrim's Way (Winchester to Canterbury) leaves off, for it provides a link of over 1,250 miles (2,000 km) between Canterbury and Rome, and was a major pilgrimage route in the Middle Ages. Only a few decades ago, the route was of interest only to scholars.

Now it has become a legitimate walking objective, passing through parts of England (Kent), France (Nord-Pas-de-Calais and Picardy), Switzerland and Italy (Piedmont, Lombardy and Tuscany), becoming designated in 2004 as a major cultural route. In Italy it is particularly noteworthy for its many churches and shrines dedicated to St Francis, including Greccio, where he is believed to have invented the first Christmas crib.

Croagh Patrick – Situated near the town of Westport, County Mayo in the Irish Republic, this is a shorter route, consisting of a 5-mile (8-km) walk originating in the village of Murrisk and culminating in the ascent of Croagh Patrick, a mountain that's 2,500 ft (762 m) above sea level and requiring a 2-hour climb. It's believed to have been a site of pilgrimage for at least 5,000 years. Its principal association, however, is with St Patrick, who reputedly fasted on the top of the mountain for 40 days and nights while battling pagan gods. It sees around 30,000 walkers climbing it on the final Sunday in July (Reek Sunday), many ascending it in bare feet as a form of penance.

El Camino de Santiago – Often simply referred to as 'El Camino' or 'The Way', this is one of the most important Christian pilgrimage routes of medieval times. It's not just one route; there are lots of them, starting at various places in Europe, all eventually converging on Santiago de Compostela in northwestern Spain, supposedly the burial place of St James, his believed remains having been found in the ninth century. It was declared the first European Culture Route by the Council of Europe in 1987 and it's been named a UNESCO World Heritage

Site. Walkers may choose to start from France, with one popular route stretching from Roncesvalles via Leon for 500 miles (800 km), or from Portugal, starting in Lisbon or Porto, but there are numerous other options. The number walking El Camino has increased greatly in recent years, from 2,491 in 1985 to nearly 280,000 in 2016.

Did you know that a film based on the El Camino route was released in 2010? Called *The Way*, it was directed by Emilio Estevez and featured his real-life father Martin Sheen. Sheen stars as an American doctor who backpacks the route in memory of his son who died while walking it, and in doing so rediscovers his sense of identity and reconnects with the son he lost. This is the principal theme of the film; and with the diverse range of characters and stunning Basque scenery, culminating in the glorious images of Santiago itself, and the atmospheric and often haunting music, it's a hugely enjoyable and enriching movie. Anyone watching it will be tempted to try the Camino for themselves.

Adam's Peak – This pilgrimage route in Sri Lanka is in fact simply a journey up this eponymous mountain, cone-shaped and 7,359 ft (2,243 m) high. The explorer Marco Polo noted it as an important place of pilgrimage, and the Arab traveller Ibn Battuta is known to have climbed to the summit in 1344. What makes it arguably unique as a pilgrimage walk is that it has links to three separate faith traditions. It's renowned for the so-called Sri Pada or Sacred Footprint, a rock formation believed to be the footprint of Buddha, Shiva or Adam. Many pilgrims choose to start their climb at 2 a.m., timing their ascent so that they reach the summit at sunrise. There are six separate trails up the mountainside.

St Paul's Trail – This 310-mile (500-km) trail in Turkey partially follows St Paul's journey to spread Christianity. Starting from Perge or Aspendos and finishing at Antioch, there is tremendous variety in the scenery: the route winds it way past pine forests, gorges, cliffs, the Taurus Mountains, pastures and the Turkish Lake District. The walk reaches a maximum altitude of 7,216 ft (2,200 m). On the way you'll see Roman and medieval roads, aqueducts, Byzantine and Ottoman settlements, churches and mosques.

Kumano Kodo – This is the name given to a series of ancient pilgrimage routes that criss-cross their way through the mountainous Japanese peninsula of Kii Hanto to the revered Kumano Sanzan Temple complex, birthplace of the Kumano cult. Although it's not a long way, roughly 25 miles (40 km) depending on your exact choice of route, it is a breathtaking journey through rugged mountain scenery, with tiny traditional wooded villages lining the route.

The Shikoku Pilgrimage – With 1,200 years of history, the Shikoku Pilgrimage runs past 88 temples along the coast of the eponymous Japanese island. Associated with the Buddhist monk Kukai, born in AD 774, the pilgrimage gives an insight into Japan's history and traditions. It's 750 miles (1,200 km) in length and can take between 30 and 60 days to complete. Many pilgrims begin their journey by visiting Mount Koya, the headquarters of Shingon Buddhism.

6 | REMARKABLE WALKERS

*'It was then well past one o'clock and I had thirty
miles to walk, with only four hours of daylight left.'*

John Merrill, *Turn Right at Land's End*

Here we identify some of the most distinguished and colourful
personalities in the world of walking – starting with three men
and one woman who have walked round the world, and ending
with one prolific walker who achieved immortality through his
written work.

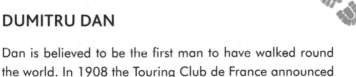

DUMITRU DAN

Dan is believed to be the first man to have walked round
the world. In 1908 the Touring Club de France announced
a contest for walking round the world, with a prize of
100,000 francs. Dumitru Dan, a Romanian, was a student
in Paris at the time, and decided to take up the challenge

with three fellow Romanian students. In 1910, wearing native dress and walking in sandals, they set off with their dog Harap. All three of Dan's companions died en route; one through opium poisoning in India in 1911, one from a mountain accident in China in 1913, and one as a result of gangrene when crossing the USA. Dan then had to put his adventure on hold due to the outbreak of World War One but finally completed it in 1923 – although the actual value of his prize had diminished massively (to less than a tenth of what it had been in 1910).

FACT FILE

Dan...

- wore out 497 pairs of shoes;

- crossed five continents and three oceans;

- visited 76 countries and over 1,500 cities;

- made it into the *Guinness Book of Records* and after his death in 1979 was buried in a Heroes' Cemetery in Romania.

DAVE KUNST

Kunst, an American, was the first person whose circumnavigation of the world was verified. He started in Waseca, Minnesota in June 1970 and finished in October 1974. He began the journey with his brother John and a mule named Willie Makeit. All went well initially; they walked to New York and, leaving the mule there, flew to Portugal (acquiring a second mule). They then crossed Europe and continued on into Afghanistan where they were attacked by bandits and John was killed. Dave survived the attack but was injured. After a four-month lay-off, he continued with another brother, Pete. Denied access to the USSR, they flew from India to Australia. Pete returned but Dave continued, with a third mule. This mule died but a Perth schoolteacher agreed to transport Dave's supplies by car. At length Kunst completed his journey, returned to Australia and married the schoolteacher. Both are still alive and together today.

FACT FILE

+ Kunst walked 20 million steps and wore out 21 pairs of shoes.

JEAN BÉLIVEAU

In 2011, the Canadian Béliveau completed the longest recorded walk around the world, measured at 47,000 miles (75,000 km), and the longest uninterrupted walk in human history. His trek began on his forty-fifth birthday in August 2000, the result, he says, of a mid-life crisis, and ended 11 years later. He stayed with 1,600 different families during his walk and visited 64 countries. Among his most vivid memories were eating snake in China and insects in Africa, being escorted by armed soldiers in the Philippines, a close encounter with a puma in a South American desert, and being kidnapped by escaped murderers.

FACT FILE

* The reason for his marathon walk was to draw attention to child victims of violence, which coincided with a United Nations initiative on this issue.

* He said the hardest part of the planning was telling his wife what he was going to do.

* He carried his equipment in a three-wheeled 'stroller'.

* He wore out 49 pairs of shoes.

* On his walk he met four Nobel Peace Prize winners, including Nelson Mandela, who told him 'the world needs people like you'.

FFYONA CAMPBELL

Born in 1967, Campbell, an Englishwoman, was the first woman to walk round the world (albeit not continuously), covering 20,000 miles (32,000 km) over 11 years, raising £180,000 for charity.

After leaving school at 16, she walked from John o'Groats to Land's End, completing the journey in 49 days; at that time she was the youngest person to have done this. At 18 she crossed the USA on foot from New York to Los Angeles, a distance of some 3,500 miles (5,600 km). Owing to illness she was unable to keep up the very demanding schedule she set for herself and, in order to avoid letting anyone down, she on three occasions accepted a lift from her back-up driver to make up time.

Determined to show she could complete a long-distance trek without missing any miles, at 21 she walked 3,200 miles (5,120 km) across Australia, covering some 50 miles (80 km) a day with no missed sections; her adventures are described in her book *Feet of Clay*. Then, starting in April 1991 in Cape Town, she walked the entire length of Africa, covering over 9,900 miles (16,000 km) and ending at Tangier in Morocco in September 1993. During her journey she had to be evacuated by the French Foreign Legion from Zaire owing to an uprising, but was able to return and continue; she then had to do an extra 2,500 miles (4,000 km) round a war zone! Her journey is described in her book *On Foot Through Africa*. Then in April 1994 she walked right through Europe, starting at Algeciras in Spain and, on returning to Britain, walking all the way up to John o'Groats. Not content with all that, she returned to the USA and this time managed to cross the continent without any lifts. This journey is described in her book *The Whole Story*.

FACT FILE

- Campbell raised money for charity by selling advertising space on her forehead.

- Inspired by hunter-gatherers she met on her walk, she lived among the Aborigines for three months and has since taught people in Britain to be hunter-gatherers.

- Born into a naval family, she attended 15 schools and as a child moved home 24 times.

'I sank down under the shower and thought: this is real! I'd imagined it so often. It was absolute, indescribable luxury.'
On Foot Through Africa

'I walked on across flat, open plains of succulent green shrubs and yellow grass, towards a far distant horizon.'
On Foot Through Africa

JOHN HILLABY

A British travel writer who was born in 1917 and died in 1996, Hillaby is remarkable for his quest to walk from Land's End to John o'Groats without using any roads at all. Although that was his avowed intention, he found it impossible because too many paths had become overgrown, enclosed, ploughed up or obstructed. The walk is described in his book *Journey Through Britain*, published in 1968 and arguably the best written account of the 'end-to-end' walk ever to have appeared in print.

'Walking is intimate: it releases something unknown in any other form of travel.'
Journey Through Britain

'Could it be that cartographers were in league with the woodsmen in an effort to confound incursonists?'
Journey Through Britain

FACT FILE

♦ Hillaby also undertook a 1,000-mile (1,600-km) walk with a camel train through northern Kenya to Lake Turkana, which he described in his book *Journey to the Jade Sea*, published in 1964.

- ◆ He also accomplished a walk across Europe, recounted in his book *Journey Through Europe*, published in 1972.

- ◆ Both these journeys were undertaken alone but in 1981 he married Kathleen Burton, who also loved walking, and she featured in his later books as his walking companion.

JOHN MERRILL

Born in London on 19 August 1943, he could be described as a professional marathon walker, active in undertaking very long walks and describing routes for readers to follow. He also lectures extensively on the subject. His walks include

Hebridean Journey – 1,003 miles (1,614 km)

Irish Island Journey – 1,578 miles (2,540 km)

Parkland Journey – 2,043 miles (3,288 km)

Land's End to John o'Groats – 1,608 miles (2,588 km)

Across the USA coast to coast – 4,226 miles (6,801 km) in 178 days

Appalachian Trail – just under 2,200 miles (3,500 km)

Pacific Crest Trail – 2,700 miles (4,300 km)

Continental Divide – 4,500 miles (7,200 km)

Le Puy to Santiago de Compostela – 1,100 miles (1,760 km)

Buckeye Trail in Ohio – 1,310 miles (2,110 km)

FACT FILE

- Merrill calculates he walked over 206,000 miles (329,600 km) between 1969 and 2013.
- His walking has raised over £750,000 for charity.
- He's author of well over 300 walking guides.
- He never carries water (don't try this at home!).
- He says the limit of endurance is 200 miles (320 km) a week.

- He's worn out 118 pairs of boots, over 1,000 pairs of socks and 43 rucksacks.

- He's also an ordained minister.

However, perhaps his greatest claim to fame is that he became the first person to walk the entire coastline of Great Britain on an almost-continuous expedition between January and November 1978. It wasn't quite continuous in that he suffered a foot fracture and had to rest for a month or so during the walk. The total mileage covered was 6,824 (10,982 km). Apart from his injury break he had only one – unscheduled – rest day (caused by bad weather) and covered the entire distance on foot, only using vehicles to convey him from his finishing point on any given day and return him back to that same point the next day. Not satisfied with walking the coastline, he incorporated climbs of Snowdon, Scafell Pike and Ben Nevis into his itinerary. He averaged 26 miles (42 km) a day with 50–60 lb (22–27 kg) of equipment; on 22 October 1978 he walked from Kings Lynn to Holkham, a distance of 39 miles (62.5 km). His extraordinary feat was chronicled in his book *Turn Right at Land's End*. Some extracts:

'I shuddered inside as the enormity of what I had achieved so far became clear.'

'With almost 2,300 miles behind me I was beginning to feel very fit.'

'To have found a wife on the walk was a bonus I had definitely not expected.'

GEORGE MEEGAN

Meegan, an Englishman born in 1952, is famous for his unbroken walk of the entire Western hemisphere, from the southern tip of South America to the northernmost part of Alaska, a distance of 19,019 miles (30,608 km). Starting in 1977 and ending in 1983, unbroken and unaided by any transport, the walk was:

The first journey on foot crossing South and Central America

The first journey on foot crossing Latin America

The first journey on foot crossing from the tropic of Capricorn via the equator to the tropic of Cancer

The first journey on foot between the equator and the Arctic Circle

The first journey on foot to connect the Southern, Atlantic, Pacific and Arctic oceans

It was also the most degrees of latitude ever covered on foot

FACT FILE

- Meegan estimates he took 31 million steps.

- He visited 14 countries.

- He was briefly imprisoned as a vagrant in Argentina.

- In 2010 he stood as an independent parliamentary candidate in the Gillingham and Rainham constituency – and came last.

> • At the end of his walk Meegan said: 'I've just lost my best friend – I've run out of road.'

WALKING AT SPEED

Race walking first appeared in the modern Olympics in 1904 as a half-mile walk in the then equivalent of the decathlon. In 1908, standalone 1,500 m and 3,000 m race walks were added, but modern Olympic events are the 20 km and 50 km race walks.

- The record for the 20 km race walk is held by Yusuke Suzuki of Japan, who accomplished the race in just over 1 hour 16 minutes in Nomi, Japan in 2015.

- The women's record for the same distance is held by Elmira Alembekova of Russia who accomplished the race in 1 hour 24 minutes in Sochi, Russia, in 2015.

- The record for the 50 km race walk is held by Yohann Diniz of France, who accomplished the race in just over 3 hours 32 minutes in Zurich, Switzerland in 2014.

- The women's record for the same distance is held by Ines Henriques of Portugal, who accomplished the race in 4 hours 5 minutes in London in 2017.

A WALKER WHO JUST KEPT GOING

Georges Holtyzer of Belgium walked 418.49 miles (619 km) in 6 days, 10 hours and 58 minutes between 19 July and 26 July 1986. He stopped only for a maximum of 2 minutes every 4 hours to change his shoes and answer the call of nature.

But we save the best walker till last......

ALFRED WAINWRIGHT

Although Wainwright never matched the aggregate distances or speeds achieved by the above, he is arguably the most famous and best-loved British walker of all, not simply because of his own achievements but because of his guidebooks, which have inspired millions of people to enjoy the same landscapes and get the same pleasure out of walking as he did.

Alfred Wainwright was born in Blackburn, Lancashire on 17 January 1907 and started work as an office boy in the town's borough engineering department, subsequently developing his career with Blackburn Borough Council, but even at a young age he walked a good deal and showed a great interest in cartography. He travelled to the Lake District for the first time in 1930 and so loved the area that he decided to move there, taking a job at the Kendal Borough Treasurers Office, where he remained until he retired in 1967. His love affair with the Lake District stayed with him for life.

Wainwright began work on his first *Pictorial Guide to the Lakeland Fells* in 1952 and completed the seventh volume 13 years later (though in 1974 he added a guide to the outlying Lakeland fells). He would use weekends and holidays for his field work and spend each evening on the writing and drawing, averaging a page a day. Initially he published his books privately but from 1963 they were published by the *Westmorland Gazette*. Later Michael Joseph and then Frances Lincoln took over publication.

The guides were unique in many respects. They were all hand drawn with no use of computer; the illustrations were actually more helpful than maps in including helpful features such as gates, stiles, sheepfolds etc to aid navigation, and the accompanying text showed a great empathy for the walker, as if he knew exactly how the walker would be feeling and what he would be experiencing at any given point in a walk. His walk descriptions are crammed with dry humour, of which some examples are given below.

Not content with guides to the Lake District, Wainwright prepared a guide to the Pennine Way – his *Pennine Way Companion*, duly updated, is still arguably the best of all the Pennine Way guides available – and in 1972 he devised his own Coast to Coast Walk (see p.134). Although this still, remarkably, lacks any 'official' status at all, it is one of the most popular walking routes in Great Britain and was once voted the second best walk in the world! He went on to produce a large number of books and television programmes, and since his death there have been numerous programmes about him and his walks. He was married twice; he divorced his first wife Ruth and in 1970 married Betty, an enthusiastic walker to whom he was devoted for the rest of his life. He died in 1991. Meanwhile his original pictorial guides have continued to sell in huge numbers; to date they've sold more than 2 million copies.

FACT FILE

- The 214 Lakeland fells described in his *Pictorial Guides* have become known as Wainwrights and visiting them all is a common form of 'peak bagging' with **many hundreds of walkers** having done the lot, one as young as five years of age.

- Most of the profits from his books went to animal welfare charities.

- His *Pennine Way Companion* describes the walk backwards, the route description beginning towards the end of the book and ending towards the start.

- He wrote in the region of 60 books and provided material for a dozen more, while around 20 books have been written about him and his work.

THE WISDOM OF ALFRED WAINWRIGHT

'Always, at Keld, there is the music of the water.'
Pennine Way Companion

'One should always have a definite
objective, in a walk as in life.'
A Coast To Coast Walk

'The best form of walking is fell walking and the
best part of fell walking is ridge walking.'
A Coast to Coast Walk

THERE OUGHT TO BE A WORD FOR IT (3)

Life-affirming and hugely walk-enhancing gastronomic
experience in on-route pub or restaurant such as
consumption of enormous bowlful of syrup sponge pudding
with lashings of custard

Having placed everything you have decided to take with
you on your walking holiday in your rucksack and zipped it
up with extreme difficulty, infuriatingly spotting small item
you're wanting to take but find is still sitting on the carpet
in your front room

Obsessive walker's pursuit of unlikely and somewhat
offbeat objective, e.g. the most northwesterly point of each
county in Great Britain or exploration on foot of all places
in Great Britain beginning with the letter Q

Virtuous feeling experienced by walker having spent their
Sunday evening re-waterproofing their walking jacket,
gelling their walking boots and correctly pairing up freshly
laundered walking socks

Disappointment that the rapport you established with the attractive stranger at the top of Ben Nevis isn't replicated when you next meet at the Tesco in-store cafe in Reading

Sensation of arriving ravenously hungry at pub or cafe at 2.16 p.m. in the course of a long walk, only to be told that 'we stop serving food at 2.15 p.m.'

Descriptive of hypnotic state in which new convert to the joys of walking spends entire evenings checking out comparison websites for the best-value boot polish

Regrettable sense of self-satisfaction on reaching hilltop in beautifully clear conditions then descending from it and meeting other walkers heading towards it just as it becomes totally enveloped in mist

Feeling of deflation you get when having completed what you regarded as a fierce climb and descent, you read a book about the same walk describing the climb as 'one which you could comfortably take your granny up after your second helping of Christmas pudding'

The act of breaking off a chunk of chocolate-coated Kendal Mint Cake onto an open page of the Wainwright guide on a cloudless golden autumn morning on a Lakeland mountainside with nobody else about and thinking it can't get any better than this

Our exploration of the joy of walking is almost over. You've learned of the many reasons why it's great to walk. You've learned how many amazing walking opportunities exist both on your own doorstep and right across Great Britain and abroad. And you'll have been inspired by the countless achievements of many amazing walkers. We wish you all the best as you embark on your own journeys of exploration and wonder! Happy walking.

APPENDIX: FURTHER READING AND INFORMATION

These days information on all aspects of walking is very easily available on the internet. Googling pretty much any name, place, subject or article mentioned above will open up literally thousands of websites and web entries. It would be pointless to list all the websites I use to get information from; there are just too many.

For traditional paper books and guides, your best bet is your local public library or bookshop, or, for information about walks in the locality, your nearest tourist information office.

I do recommend a number of books, some of which sadly are out of print but which you may be able to get from the library, from a second-hand bookseller or on eBay!

Ffyona Campbell – *On Foot Through Africa* (Orion, 1994) – Campbell's account of her astonishing, courageous and inspiring African journey, against all the odds, from Cape Town to Tangier

John Merrill – *Turn Right at Land's End* (Oxford Illustrated Press, 1980) – Merrill's account, in diary form, of his epic coast walk in 1978

John Hillaby – *Journey Through Britain* (Constable, 1968) – arguably the definitive account of the end-to-end walk, beautifully written

Alfred Wainwright – *Pictorial Guide to Lakeland Fells* (Frances Lincoln, various) – quite simply, the best walking guidebooks ever written

Alfred Wainwright – *Pennine Way Companion* (2nd edition, Frances Lincoln, 2012) – still regarded as the definitive work on the subject

Alfred Wainwright – *A Coast to Coast Walk* (2nd edition, Frances Lincoln, 2010) – much revised since the original appeared, but a true labour of love

H. D. Westacott – *The Walker's Handbook* (Footpath Publications, latest edition 2015) – full of very practical advice for walkers of all levels of experience

Paddy Dillon – *The National Trails* (Cicerone, 2007) – an at-a-glance guide to Britain's primary long-distance routes, superbly illustrated

The UK Trailwalkers' Handbook (Cicerone, 2013) – a guide to almost every named path in Britain – enough walking for several lifetimes

Alan Plowright – *Plowright Follows Wainwright* (Michael Joseph, 1995) – an inspiring, very readable and amusing account of a Yorkshireman's discovery of the joy of walking

Sinclair McKay – *Ramble On* (Fourth Estate, 2012) – an excellent recent social history of walking for pleasure

David Bathurst – *Walking the County High Points of England* (Summersdale, 2012) – a guide to scaling every county summit, varying hugely in difficulty and terrain

David Bathurst – *The Walker's Year* (Summersdale, 2015) – a handbook bursting with tips, facts and folklore to guide those who love to roam through the natural rhythms and seasons of the year

TOM
CHESSHYRE

FROM
SOURCE
TO SEA

Notes from a
215-MILE WALK
along the
RIVER THAMES

FROM SOURCE TO SEA
Notes from a 215-Mile Walk along the River Thames

Tom Chesshyre

ISBN: 978-1-78685-286-1

Paperback

£9.99

Over the years, authors, artists and amblers aplenty have felt the pull of the Thames, and now travel writer Tom Chesshyre is following in their footsteps.

He's walking the length of the river from the Cotswolds to the North Sea – a winding journey of over two hundred miles. Join him for an illuminating stroll past meadows, churches and palaces, country estates and council estates, factories and dockyards. Setting forth in the summer of Brexit, and meeting a host of interesting characters along the way, Chesshyre explores the living present and remarkable past of England's longest and most iconic river.

THE
BIG WALKS
OF THE NORTH

Including: The Pennine Way, The Coast to Coast Walk,
Hadrian's Wall Path, The Cleveland Way,
The West Highland Way, The Great Glen Way

DAVID BATHURST

THE BIG WALKS OF THE NORTH

David Bathurst

ISBN: 978-1-84953-023-1

Paperback

£8.99

From the Great Glen Way to the Coast to Coast Path, there is no better way to discover the spectacular diversity of northern Britain's landscape than on foot. Whether you enjoy exploring green and gently rolling dales or tackling rugged mountain paths, there are walks here to keep you rambling all year round.

An indefatigable walker, David Bathurst has unlaced his boots to produce this invaluable and definitive companion to the ten best-loved long-distance footpaths in the north of Britain, with each split into manageable sections. Combining practical, detailed descriptions with an appreciation of the beauty and history of the British countryside, this in an indispensable guide for both experienced and novice walkers alike.

Have you enjoyed this book?
If so, why not write a review on your favourite website?

If you're interested in finding out more about our books,
find us on Facebook at **Summersdale Publishers**
and follow us on Twitter at **@Summersdale**.

Thanks very much for buying this Summersdale book.

www.summersdale.com